Ryukyu and Okinawa Environment
A History

Author
King Houghton

Copyright Notice

Copyright © 2017 Global Print Digital
All Rights Reserved

Digital Management Copyright Notice. This Title is not in public domain, it is copyrighted to the original author, and being published by **Global Print Digital**. No other means of reproducing this title is accepted, and none of its content is editable, neither right to commercialize it is accepted, except with the consent of the author or authorized distributor. You must purchase this Title from a vendor who's right is given to sell it, other sources of purchase are not accepted, and accountable for an action against. We are happy that you understood, and being guided by these terms as you proceed. Thank you

First Printing: 2017.

ISBN: 978-1-912483-55-6

Publisher: Global Print Digital.
Arlington Row, Bibury, Cirencester GL7 5ND
Gloucester
United Kingdom.
Website: www.homeworkoffer.com
.

Table of Content

Introduction 1
Ryukyu and Okinawa History 4
   Ancient Ryukyus 6
      Establishment of a Unified Royal Court 6
         The Formation of the Ryukyuan Cultural Sphere 6
         The Emergence of the Aji Feudal Chieftains and the Gusuku Castle Period 6
         What exactly is a "Gusuku"? 8
         The Royal Lineage of Myth and Legend 8
         The Legend of Minamoto Tametomo 10
         The Legend of Hagoromo or Celestial Robe 11
         King Satto and the Three Kingdoms Period 13
         The Emergence of Sho Hashi 14
         The Kadeshiga Legend 15
         The First Sho Dynasty 16
         The Construction of Ryutan Pond 17
         The Gosamaru - Amawari Revolt 17
   The Ryukyu Islands in the Age of Great Trade 18
         The Chinese Envoy System and Sovereignty 20
         Tribute and Trade: The dispatch of vassals to China 21
         Trade with Southeast Asia 23
         The Portuguese View of the Ryukyus 24
         Trade with Korea 26
         Trade with Japan 27
   Establishment of the Ryukyu Kingdom 28
         The Second Sho Dynasty 28
         The Government of King Sho Shin 30
         Construction and Cultural Enterprises 31
         Rivalry of the Sakishima Warlords 32
         Oyake-Akahachi Rebellion 33
   The Later Period Ryukyu 35
      Shimazu Invasion of the Ryukyus 36
         Relations between Toyotomi Hideyoshi, the Shimazu Clan and the Ryukyu Kingdom 36
         The Shimazu Invasion 37
         Shimazu Hegemony 39

- Establishing the Kingdom of the Ryukyus 39
- Jana Ekata Teido 40
- The Fifteen Articles 40
- A "Foreign Country" within Japan 42
- Tributary Trade Under Shimazu Hegemony 42
- Kelp and Okinawa 44
- Reconstruction of the Ryukyu Kingdom 45
  - Reforms of Haneji Choshu 45
  - The Ideas of Haneji Choshu 46
  - Construction of the Administrative Structure 47
  - Establishment of the Class System 48
  - The Reforms of Saion 49
  - Conditions in Rural Agricultural Villages 51
  - The Devastation in the Agricultural Villages 53
  - The Conditions of Rule in the Sakishima Islands 54
  - Per Capita Taxation 55
  - The Meiwa Tsunami 55
- The Flourishing Industry and Culture of the Latter Period Ryukyus 57
  - Agricultural Developments 57
  - Arts and Crafts Development 58
  - Construction of Transportation Networks 58
  - The culture in latter period of Ryukyus 59
  - Culture of the Latter Ryukyu Kingdom 60
  - Latter Period Ryukyuan Developments in Academics and Literature 62
  - Ryukyuan Culture in the Latter Period Ryukyus 64
  - Culture of the Latter Period Ryukyus 65
  - Ryukyuan Culture of the Early Modern Age (Arts and Crafts) 66
  - Latter Period Ryukyuan Culture (Residential Housing) 68

Prehistory of Okinawa 69
- The Paleolithic Age in Okinawa 71
  - The Origin of the Ryukyu Island Chain 71
  - Paleolithic Humans and Culture of the Ryukyu Archipelago 72
  - The Yamashita Dojin and Minatogawa Humans 73
  - Fossil Humans and Paleolithic Culture 74
- The Neolithic Age in Okinawa 76
  - The Neolithic Age Cultural Spheres 76
  - Aspects of Jomon Period Okinawa (1) 77
  - Aspects of Jomon Period Okinawa (2) 78
  - Aspects of Yayoi Period Okinawa 79

  The Neolithic Age in Sakishima 79
    Aspects of Neolithic Period Sakishima.. 79
    The Shell Road 81
Modern Okinawa *82*
  The Disposition of the Ryukyus 84
    Landfall of American and European Ships on the Ryukyus 86
    The Establishment of the Ryukyu Domain................................... 88
    Dissolution of the Domains and Establishment of the Prefectures........ 89
    The Ryukyus and Okinawa 91
    The Miyako and Yaeyama Separation from Okinawa................... 92
  Okinawa's Civil Rights Movement 93
    The Farmers Movements.. 95
    The Movement to Abolish the Per Capita Tax.............................. 96
    Noboru Jahana and the Prefectural Government Reform Movement.... 98
  Reformation of Old Customs and Abolition of Special Institutions............ 100
    Regional Political Reform and National Government Participation 102
    The Implementation of a Conscript Military 103
    Education and Academics in Modern Okinawa......................... 105
    The Society and Culture of Modern Okinawa............................ 107
  Life in Okinawa During the "Cycad Hell" 109
    Okinawa Social Movement 112
    The Dialect Controversy and Imperialist Education 113
  The Battle of Okinawa 114
    The Start of the Battle of Okinawa 116
    Progress of the Battle of Okinawa 118
    War on the Sakishima and Other Island Groups......................... 120
Post-War Okinawa *121*
  Defeat and U.S. Occupation 123
    The Start of U.S. Occupation 123
    Various Postwar... 124
    The Start of Postwar Government... 126
    Life under the U.S. Occupation... 128
  USCAR and the Struggle for Autonomous Rights 129
    The Policy of Maj. Gen. Sheets and the Treaty of San Francisco........... 129
    The Establishment of the Government of the Ryukyus....................... 131
    Okinawa as a Strategic Base 132
    The Price Report and the Island-wide Struggles........................ 134
  The Rise of the Popular Movement and Reversion 135
    Damage from the Bases and Okinawan Human Rights 135

The Rise of the People 136
  The Development of the Popular Movement 138
  Close of the Return to Japan Movement and Okinawan Reversion 139
  Okinawan Culture under U.S. Military Rule 140
  The Phases of Pre-Reversion Okinawa 142
 The New Life of Okinawa 144
  Rebirth of Okinawa Prefecture 144
  Special Reversion Measures and Life of the Prefectural Citizens 145
 Keywords in Postwar Okinawa 147
Tourism in Okinawa Information 162

Introduction

Okinawa Prefecture, an archipelago of 160 islands between Kyushu and Taiwan, seems like its own country. Maybe that's because once upon a time, it *was* its own kingdom the Ryukyu Kingdom with dynasties and castles (constructed mostly btw. the 14th-18th c.), as well as its own languages, culture, and cuisine. Although it was invaded by Satsuma (in what is now Kagoshima in southern Kyushu) in the early 1600s, the Ryukyu Kingdom retained domestic autonomy, trading freely with China and elsewhere, until it was annexed to Japan after the 1868 Meiji Restoration; in 1879 it was renamed Okinawa Prefecture.

You might know Okinawa as a site of brutal combat during World War II (several sites and memorials recount the horrific battle and massive casualties). If you're a diver, you might know Okinawa as one of the best diving spots in the world. But what I've always liked about Okinawa apart from its unique museums, historic sites, tropical weather, and the finest beaches I've seen in Japan is its laid-back, rural atmosphere. In fact, parts of Okinawa are so off the beaten path, they seem like they're caught in a time warp of a few decades past.

Of Okinawa's 160 islands (part of the Ryukyu Island chain), only 40 some are inhabited. The largest, Okinawa Island (Okinawa-honto), is home to Naha, capital of Okinawa Prefecture and gateway to the rest of the islands by sea and by air. After visiting Okinawa Island's many attractions, you might wish to fly or take a ferry onward to one or more of my other favorites, like Kume Island, renowned for its beaches, sugar cane fields, and historic sites relating to the Ryukyu Kingdom. Iriomote is famous for its vast pristine wilderness and for scuba diving.

Okinawa Island

1,539km (956 miles) SW of Tokyo

On April 1, 1945, Allied forces landed on Okinawa Island in an attempt to seize control of the island and use it as a base for an invasion of mainland Japan. The Battle of Okinawa, the only land battle on Japanese territory, raged for the next 82 days, with many Japanese troops and drafted Okinawans, including high-school students, ensconced in the island's many caves. By the time the horrific fighting was over, more than 200,000 people had lost their lives. Just a few weeks later, after atomic bombs were dropped on Hiroshima and Nagasaki, the Japanese surrendered.

Okinawa was then placed under control of the U.S. government until 1972, when sovereignty reverted back to Japan. Remaining, however, are American military bases, which were greatly expanded during the Korean War and that occupy land that had belonged to Okinawans for generations (75% of American bases in Japan are in Okinawa). Many protests have been lodged against the U.S. presence, especially following rapes of local women and girls by U.S. servicemen; as part of ongoing negotiations, some 8,000 troops will transfer from Okinawa to Guam in 2014.

Okinawa Island has a number of sites and attractions that make a 2- or 3-day stay particularly worthwhile, including nine castle sites dating from the Ryukyu Kingdom era that are on the UNESCO World Heritage list, a world-class aquarium, a theme park containing Japan's second-longest limestone cave and exhibits related to Okinawa history and culture, and several memorials for victims of the Battle of Okinawa. There are also more lighthearted pursuits, including shopping and dining in downtown Naha, sunning and swimming on the island's many white sandy beaches, and snorkeling and scuba diving among the island's surrounding coral reefs.

Ryukyu and Okinawa History

The Ancient Ryukyus generally refers to the period from the 12th century, at the beginning of the Gusuku (Castle) Period, through to the establishment of the Ryukyu Kingdom, to the invasion of the Ryukyus by the Shimazu Clan from Kyushu in 1609.

In 12th century Okinawa, the long Shell Mound period, where people lived a hunter-gatherer lifestyle, was coming to an end as an agrarian society was formed. In conjunction with this, regional chieftains, called Aji, gathered political power in their respective areas, built castles, called Gusuku, for fortresses and struggles for overall political power began. This is called the Gusuku Period.

By the 14th century three great houses had developed and Okinawa was divided into three centers of power; the south, called Nanzan, the central area, called Chuzan, and the north, called Hokuzan. This was called the Sanzan or Three Kingdoms Period. The kingdoms had good ports and started to conduct active trading with China to increase their economic power.

In the 15th century one of the leaders from the south, Sho Hashi, succeeded in unifying the three kingdoms. The Ryukyu Kingdom was born.

The Ryukyu Kingdom built up trading relationships with China, East Asia, Korea, Japan, and other neighboring Asian and East Asian nations. This era has been called The Great Age of Trade.

The First Ryukyu Dynasty founded by Sho Hashi was succeeded by the Second Ryukyu Dynasty. Among the greatest of the kings was King Sho Shin, the third to ascend the throne in the second dynasty. During his reign, the kingdom was thoroughly organized, power was centralized and many construction projects were carried out. Sho Shin's reign is suitably called the Golden Age of the Ryukyus.

During the Ancient Ryukyu period, Okinawa received influences from Japan and Asia. It experienced a blossoming of its own distinctive history and culture while forming and developing itself as an independent nation. But in 1609, due to a military invasion by the Shimazu Clan, the kingdom functionally lost its independence as a sovereign nation and became closely tied to the Shogunate system in Japan.

Ancient Ryukyus
Establishment of a Unified Royal Court
The Formation of the Ryukyuan Cultural Sphere

From the time corresponding to the Jomon (to 200 BC) and Yayoi (200 BC to 250 AD) periods to the Late Heian period (897-1185 AD) on the mainland of Japan, the islands of the Ryukyu chain developed an independent culture and history with qualities distinctive from the Japanese.

From the 12th to the 15th centuries, the islands entered the Gusuku (Castle) era and the Ryukyus became a unified cultural sphere with the creation of the Ryukyu Kingdom. The background to these developments was the tremendous changes carried out in the East Asian region surrounding Okinawa.

During the 14th century, China assumed a central role in East Asia and a new order within the region was established. Adjacent countries, including Japan, began trading relationships. Many ships traveled in and out of Okinawa via the close-by East China Sea. The Ryukyu chain of islands became a place where merchants came and went as they pursued their trading.

The Emergence of the Aji Feudal Chieftains and the Gusuku Castle Period

The Gusuku (Castle) Period extended from the 12th to the 15th centuries as the economies of the islands shifted from hunter-gather to agrarian lifestyles and they began to produce iron utensils.

The population migrated inland to level ground suitable for farming and formed villages. As the stable agrarian lifestyle brought prosperity, these villages began to increase in size and became village communities. The communities became active in trading with foreign countries, with the leaders in each region actively seeking trading relationships.

Through this process, feudal leaders, called Aji, accumulated power and wealth. These lords built fortifications, called Gusuku, and began to rule over adjacent areas . As time went on disputes over power broadened.

By the 14th century power became even more centralized in supreme lords called Yononushi. The main island of Okinawa was divided into 3 regions; the northern, central, and southern areas, and large castles were constructed in each of these regions. Each area became, in effect, a small sovereign nation. Thus started the Sanzan or Three Kingdoms Period.

By the end of the Gusuku era, in the 15th century, the strongest of the Aji lords, a man named Sho Hashi, managed to consolidate the three kingdoms and the first unified nation in the Ryukyus was born.

What exactly is a "Gusuku"?

The Okinawa word Gusuku is written with the Chinese character for castle and generally refers to a castle or fortification. However, due to the diversity of the form and function in the areas that use this designation, the genuine etymology of this word is still controversial.

So far the historical references have frequently referred to a Gusuku as the place where an Aji chieftain lived. There are, however, theories that state that the essence of the word indicates a stone enclosed sacred precinct and another which theorizes that it refers to an enclosure built for protection by the early villagers. Whether it is simply a stone enclosure or an accented way of saying Ushuku, or place to stay, there are diverse theories as the origin of the word.

As it is yet to be fully elucidated and yet occupies a substantial place within the history of the Ryukyus, new research is eagerly awaited which will solve the mystery of these ancient ruins.

The Royal Lineage of Myth and Legend

The dawn of the history of the Ryukyus, and the origin and succession of each member of the royal line were written down in three formal histories that were compiled by the monarchy; the Chuzan Seikan, the Chuzan Seifu, and the Kyuyo.

According to these histories a god, Amamiku / Amamikiyo, came to the world below and created the islands and let the first man and woman live on them. Three sons and two daughters were born to them. The first son became king, the second son became an Aji (regional feudal lord) and the third son a farmer. The eldest daughter became the Ufujimi, or high priestess, for the whole country and the second daughter became a Noro, or regional priestess.

The king was called Tenson and during his long reign he divided Okinawa into three regions, taught the people how to farm and build houses, named the royal abode Shuri and classified the government administration into sections. While obviously a legend, the content gives important clues to historians regarding the historical awareness of the age.

According to the histories, Shunten succeeded Tenson and ruled from the middle 12th to 13th centuries. Legend has it that Shunten was the son of Minamoto Tametomo, a famous Heian period exile from mainland Japan forced to live his life out in the remote islands. It must be stressed here that this is legend and its foundation in truth has been denied.

Next in the royal line came Eiso, who ruled from the middle 13th century until the middle 14th century. According to the histories, Eiso's mother had a dream in which the sun gave this child to her and so Eiso is called Tidanufa (child of the sun). Eiso is credited with ruling the country using a gusuku (castle) as his base of power and improving developments in agriculture, as well as his calm and steady way of ruling. While the legendary accounts of King Eiso are of his being born as the child of the sun, he is also written about in some ballads so it is thought that he might have actually have existed, although this is unconfirmed.

The Legend of Minamoto Tametomo

There is a legend recorded in the history compiled by the Ryukyu royal court that King Shunten was the son of the Japanese Heian period exile Minamoto Tametomo.

The story goes that Tametomo was exiled to Izu, Oshima Island after his loss in the Hogen (Imperial regency) disturbances in medieval Japan. When he tried to escape exile, he was washed ashore in the northern part of the Ryukyus by the current and by fate of heaven landed in Nakijin. For this reason the port in the area is called Untenko (fate of heaven harbor). Tametomo moved to the southern part of Okinawa and married the daughter of the Ozato Aji (chieftain) and had a son by her. He later returned home alone to the Japanese mainland, leaving his wife and son behind. His wife and son waited long and faithfully for him to return at a location near a harbor which bears the name Machinato (Makiminato), or "waiting harbor". The son went on to be King Shunten.

While it seems like a simple fable, its historical context is of note. In the 17th century the Shimazu Clan of Kyushu used this story as one of the necessary justifications for the subordination and invasion of the Ryukyus. In other words the Tokugawa Shogunate used the rationale that the Ryukyu kings, the Tokugawa family and the Shimazu Clan had a common ancestor within the Minamoto line and thus the Ryukyus could then simply be incorporated into the Shogunate system of Japan.

It was by this design that the story of Tametomo came to be written into the very first history of the Ryukyu Kingdom.

The Legend of Hagoromo or Celestial Robe

After King Eiso came King Satto and the following is legend told about him.

There was once a poor farmer who lived in Urasoe named Okuma Ufuya. At the Mori-no Kawa spring he chanced to see a beautiful celestial maiden who came to the spring to bathe. Okuma Ufuya hid her cloak so she could not return to heaven and then offered her refuge in his house. As time passed they became husband and wife and she bore a son and daughter. The son he named Janamoi. Finally one day the celestial maiden chanced to find the cloak again and returned to heaven.

The son, renowned for his virtue, grew up and eventually married the daughter of the Katsuren area Aji. One day he came upon a nugget of gold which he sold to buy iron farming tools for the village and divided among the village farmers. The village became prosperous and he was renowned throughout the country. Gaining the trust of the people, he became King Satto.

In a way similar to Shunten and Eiso, Satto's emergence into the noble lineage is brought about by an extraordinary fate, which he uses to innovate the age into which he was born. The history of the early kings is tinged with these kind of extraordinary occurrences.

King Satto and the Three Kingdoms Period

According to the histories, King Eiso's monarchy was disrupted and the Ryukyus divided into three spheres of power and influence. This started the Three Kingdoms Period. The king who had succeeded King Eiso to power in the middle kingdom called Chuzan was King Satto. The legend that he was the son of a celestial maid and a poor farmer, born under an extraordinary good fate, gave Satto an air of divinity.

Satto of Chuzan was the proudest of his power among the three kingdoms' rulers. This led him to start relations with Ming Dynasty China as a tributary nation, sending the first tribute ship to the Ming emperor in 1372 AD. Through this the Ryukyus developed a formal trading relationship with China. In return for agreeing to a suzerain relationship under China, King Satto and the other kingdoms' rulers, Sho Satto from the southern kingdom Nanzan and Haniji from the northern kingdom Hokuzan, received recognition from the Emperor of China and legitimized themselves as rulers of their respective nations. In this way China tied the nations of East Asia together in a hierarchy with China at the top. This system was called Sappo and tribute was offered to China by the nations and in return received the honor of trade with the Chinese.

Intense rivalry developed between the kingdoms and they began using castles as their base of operations. The Hokuzan castle was named Nakijin Gusuku, the Chuzan castle was named Urasoe Gusuku and the Nanzan castle was named Shimajiri Ozato Gusuku. From the beginning of the 14th century to the start of the 15th century, the era was called the Sanzan, or Three Kingdoms Period. During this time, trade with other countries increased the economic power of the islands and set the stage for the formation of a united Ryukyu Kingdom.

The Emergence of Sho Hashi

It was Sho Hashi, from the southern part of Okinawa, that finally brought the whole of the Ryukyus under the control of a single ruler for the first time. Using the excellent Baten harbor and Yonabaru as his base, Sho Hashi accumulated the financial resources through trade which enabled him to achieve his ambitions.

In 1406 Sho Hashi and his father Shisho attacked and took the Urasoe Gusuku of Chuzan. Solidifying his base by installing his father as king of Chuzan, Satto began preparations to unify the Ryukyus.

In 1422 he took the Hokuzan castle Nakijin Gusuku, in 1429 he destroyed Nanzan's castle, Shimajiri Ozato Gusuku. For the next 450 years the Ryukyu monarchy stood unified. In this way the First Ryukyu Dynasty began.

During this time it is said that Sho Hashi transferred his base of operations to Shuri Gusuku from Urasoe Gusuku, in what is now called Naha City , but the details of this move are not well known. However, it is recorded that in 1427 a Chinese named Kaiki was commissioned by Sho Hashi to construct Ryutan Pond and Ankokuzan (a park area). Shurijo Castle became the symbol of the monarchy and the town of Shuri became a bustling castle town.

The Kadeshiga Legend

In the Ozato area of present day Itoman City there was an abundant small river called Kadeshiga. The following legend is told about this place.

Kadeshiga was known among the farming folk of Nanzan as a river which brought blessings and was a reliable source of much needed water. Sho Hashi, later to conquer Chuzan and become king, offered the rather greedy Nanzan king Tarumi a golden folding screen in exchange for this water source. Tarumi was glad to make the exchange but it caused a problem for those that used the spring, the farming folk of Ozato.

Sho Hashi then allowed only those that followed him use of the spring, which of course meant that the people of the area soon began to support Sho Hashi. King Tarumi, having lost the trust of the people, was soon easily defeated by Sho Hashi.

The First Sho Dynasty

The First Sho Dynasty was established in 1406 by Sho Hashi and lasted for 64 years through seven successions of kings.

During this dynasty a long bank connecting to the harbor in Naha with Shuri was built as well as Ryutan Pond, Buddhist temples and shrines, and the casting of the Bankoku Shinryo-no-Kane (Bridge Between Nations) Bell. All of this made Shuri the symbol of the Ryukyu Kingdom.

The tributary state relationship created by King Satto opened the way for thriving trade with the countries of East and Southeast Asia and developed as an important policy in promoting the Ryukyu Kingdom overseas.

Genealogy of the First Sho Dynasty

King	Reign	Years on the Throne
Sho Shisho	1406-1421	16 years
Sho Hashi	1422-1439	18 years

Sho Chu	1440-1444	5 years
Sho Shitatsu	1445-1449	5 years
Sho Kinbuku	1450-1453	4 years
Sho Taikyu	1454-1460	7 years
Sho Toku	1461-1469	9 years

The Construction of Ryutan Pond

Ryutan Pond, located near Shurijo Castle, is an artificial pond constructed in 1427 by the prime minister of the Ryukyu Kingdom, Kaiki, under orders of the second king of the First Sho Dynasty, King Sho Hashi. On Ryutan Pond the investiture envoys from China were entertained by such events as the Haari Dragon boat races.

During the kingdom period many fish swam in the pond and flowers and trees were planted around it. With Shurijo Castle reflecting off the surface of the pond, it was said to be the most beautiful sight in the kingdom

The Gosamaru - Amawari Revolt

The First Sho Dynasty succeeded in unifying the Ryukyus but it was, unfortunately, politically unstable. During the dynasty there were a number of revolts such as the Gosamaru / Amawari Revolt.

For his role in the conquest of the Hokuzan kingdom with Sho Hashi, a man named Gosamaru was given rule over the central part of the Okinawa mainland during the reign of King Sho Taikyu (1454-1460).

Around that time an ambitious man named Amawari had gained power on the Katsuren Peninsula. King Sho Taikyu arranged a strategic marriage between Amawari and his daughter Momotofumi Agari, but it failed to appease ambitions. Amawari informed King Sho Taikyu that Gosamaru, the Aji (regional ruler) of Nakagusuku, was planning to usurp the king, and sought permission from the king to attack Gosamaru. Amawari then planned to attack the king himself. But Princess Momotohumi Agari and a vassal named Oni Ogusuku saw through his plan and Amawari and Katsuren Castle were destroyed.

This is as far as the official history records go, but there is much unknown and various opinions about what really took place.

The Ryukyu Islands in the Age of Great Trade

In the 10th to the 14th centuries in East Asia, merchants became increasingly active in trade between countries. Chinese merchants began to reside abroad in other East Asian countries for short terms to conduct trading. In Japan, the merchants of Kyushu and Seto conducted trade aggressively and enlarged their power. In this type of international atmosphere, the Three Kingdoms in Okinawa competed intensely and repeatedly with each other, finally achieving unity with the birth of the Ryukyu Kingdom. Throughout East Asia during this period countries emerged from confusion to reform and unification.

In 1368 the Ming Dynasty was established in China. The Ming, aiming to establish an international order with China as its center, called on neighboring countries to establish tributary relationships with China and established a trade embargo which prohibited free trade. In effect this policy instituted China as the leader and defined the position of neighboring countries. Only those that swore allegiance to the Ming Dynasty were given permission to engage in the lucrative trade with China by the Ming emperor. This is called the Sappo system in Japanese and by adhering to it, leaders in the neighboring countries legitimized their rule and received the benefits of trade with the more advanced China. The Three Kingdoms in Okinawa were also invited and joined in this type of relationship with China.

The Ryukyus played an important role as an intermediary trader in this system by importing the fine trade goods from China and exporting them to other Asian nations. At the same time it collected products from Japan and East Asia for the trade with China. It built a vast system of trade routes on the seas to exchange goods with other countries.

The Chinese Envoy System and Sovereignty

The Sappo, or investiture, legitimized the rule of kings of neighboring countries by the Emperor of China. In order to conduct the investiture ceremony for the newly enthroned kings, the Chinese emperor would dispatch envoys in his name to specified countries.

The first instance of their being dispatched to the Ryukyu islands is said to have been in 1396 for the enthronement of the Hokuzan king Hanachi and in 1404 for the investiture of King Bunei. After that, for close to 500 years until the time of the investiture of the last Ryukyuan King Sho Tai, the Sappo investiture system was continued.

A single envoy group would consist of 400 people and would stay in the Ryukyus for up to six months. The duties of the envoys included attendance at the official funeral for the deceased king and the enthronement ceremony for the new king. These rites were carried out on the courtyard area of Shurijo Castle called the Una and their magnificence reflected the expectations of the kings which hosted them. In other words, the authority of the king was shown to the envoys who would report this to the Chinese emperor. The kings did this in order to maintain and receive the trade monopoly they enjoyed with China and to expand their economic power. In fact the envoys brought with them many goods from China and by obtaining these the royal government enjoyed its success as an intermediary trade country with the whole of East Asia.

Pictured at right is a portion of a pictorial scroll depicting a procession of Chinese envoys on their way to an investiture ceremony at Shurijo Castle for the new king of the Ryukyus. The whole scroll is 22.5 meters and shows the procession being composed of 380 Ryukyuans and 220 Chinese Sappo envoys. In all a total of 600 persons participated in this event. From the Okinawa Prefectural Museum Collection

Tribute and Trade: The dispatch of vassals to China

The countries involved as suzerain nations under China offered tribute to the Chinese emperor, politely referred to as a kind of "gift" to China. In Japanese this tribute was called either "Shinkou" or "Chokou."

In the Ryukyu Islands, the Chuzan King Satto was the first to participate in this type of relationship with the Chinese, followed by the competing kings from the Nanzan and Hokuzan kingdoms. When the islands were unified as the Ryukyu Kingdom under Sho Hashi, the monopoly they enjoyed under this tributary trade relationship enabled rapid development in economic power for the kingdom.

The groups of vassals dispatched to China for trade and tribute numbered 300 people and ships were dispatched about once every two years. The vassals dispatched to China were permitted an audience with the emperor during which they presented letters from the Ryukyuan king and tribute goods. In exchange they received letters from the emperor to the Ryukyuan king and many high quality Chinese products.

The tribute offered to the emperor consisted of Okinawan goods including horses, sulfur, shell products, and Bashofu banana cloth fabric as well as crafts goods from Japan and rare products from Southeast Asia. The tribute brought in from the Ryukyus was of great military value to the Chinese and so the Ryukyu Kingdom was regarded as an important supply country. Moreover. because of the enthusiasm with which they engaged in the tribute and trading system, they were received warmly by their Chinese hosts compared with other countries. Gradually, the Ryukyu Kingdom was designated by China as the intermediary trader in East Asia and Southeast Asia.

Trade with Southeast Asia

The old Ryukyuan designation for Southeast Asia was "Manaban". It is not known exactly when trade with Southeast Asia began, but it was being carried out by the 14th century.

It reached full swing during the 15th century. The Ryukyu Kingdom, having obtained large quantities of superior Chinese products, brought them to their customers in Japan and Korea, acting as intermediary traders. Finally, seeking even more profits they expanded their trading routes to include the remote Southeast Asian areas.

Their trading partners were the port cities of Southeast Asia and included the then prosperous kingdoms of Siam (Thailand), Palembang (southeast Sumatra), Java (Indonesia), and Malacca (Malaysia). From the Ryukyus they brought the trade goods they obtained in China, such as ceramics and silk fabrics, as well as other products, including sulfur, from the Ryukyus and craft goods from Japan. They traded for the high quality dyes (soboku), pepper, liquors, elephant ivory, and other precious products from Southeast Asia.

However, as the Europeans countries, such as Portugal and Spain, began to exercise power in the area during the 16th century, this trade rapidly declined. As the Chinese edicts restricting trade were gradually relaxed and the merchant ships of Japan began to make their appearance, the age of competitive international commerce began in Southeast Asia.

The Ryukyu kingdom, possessing but a small amount of trading power, sent its last mission to Siam in 1570.

The numbers of trading missions dispatched to Southeast Asia.

Destination	Trading Period	Number of Ships	Destination	Trading Period	Number of Ships
Siam	1419 - 1570	62 (4)	Palembang	1428 - 1440	4
Java	1430 - 1442	6	Malacca	1463 - 1511	20 (3)
Sumatra	1463 - 1468	3	Patany	1490 - 1543	11
Anam	1509	1	Sunda	1513 - 1518	2

Created with reference to "The Ryukyuan Age" by Kurayoshi Takara
The numbers in ( ) reflect those ships which were shipwrecked.

The Portuguese View of the Ryukyus

During the Great Age of Trade, the Ryukyus were active in Southeast Asia and came to be well known even with the European traders as the Lequios or the Goresu. The impression of the Portuguese who came into contact with the Ryukyuan traders is recorded in the following material.

The men of Lequios are called Gores. They are known by either of these names but Lequios is more commonly used. The nation is a monarchy and all are without religion. Their king is subordinate to the Chinese emperor and pays him tribute. Their island is large and heavily populated. They have a particular style of ships. They possess 3 or 4 Chinese style junks but these they have been bought from the Chinese. Aside from this they have no other kinds of ships. These people conduct business with China and Malacca. Sometimes they handle business together with the Chinese and also sometimes travel on their own to the harbor of Fukien and conduct business there. Fukien is on the Chinese mainland near Canton and about a day and night, by sea, from there. The Malay and Malaccans say there is no difference between Portuguese and the Lequios except they do not buy women as Portuguese do. .

As for their land, they are said to have but wheat, rice and their own liquor and meat. The seas there are abundant in fish. As we ourselves talk of Milan and those from there, the Chinese and other peoples talk of the Lequios. They are very truthful men. They do not buy slaves, nor would they sell one of their own men for the whole world. They would die over this. They are white men, better than the Chinese and more dignified. They sail to China and take merchandise that goes from Malacca to China, and from Japan. This is an island about 7 or 8 days by sea from their island. There they buy the gold and copper in exchange for goods. The Lequios are men who freely extend credit for their merchandise. And when they come to collect their payments, should they be lied to, they collect with sword in hand.

Tome Perez "Diary of Travel in the Countries of the East"

Excerpted form "The Great Age of Navigation" Vol. V (Japanese translation by Shigeru Ikuta, Eiichi Kato, and Shinjiro Nagaoka)

Trade with Korea

Trade between the Ryukyus and Korea began in 1389 when King Satto of Chuzan dispatched an envoy to Korea. The objective of the first dispatch was to return Koreans who had been liberated from Japanese pirates (this was during the Korai Dynasty in Korea) to their native land. The Koreans returned the courtesy by sending an ambassador and the relationship continued to grow.

To reach Korea the Ryukyuan ships sailed to the Amami Islands, up the west coast of Kyushu, through Tsushima via Pusan and then towards their destination. Strictly speaking, trade ships did not head from Korea to the Ryukyus due the danger of many pirates on the coastal areas of Korea. However, the two countries built a relationship based on trust and many goods such as cotton fabrics, Korean ginseng, and Buddhist scripture were given to the Ryukyuans.

But in the mid 15th century the number of ships sailing from the Ryukyus to the Korean peninsula decreased because of incidents where Japanese merchants misrepresented themselves as Ryukyuan missions.

Trade with Japan

The Ryukyus enjoyed a privileged status as intermediary traders in the eyes of the Chinese because they accepted the suzerain relationship with China and received their envoys. This enabled the Ryukyus to develop as an economic power. The Japanese, then called the Yamato, held a particular importance to Ryukyuans because of their relations with China. Specialty goods were rare in the Ryukyus and many of the tribute items presented to the Chinese were obtained by the Ryukyuans in Japan. Japan also fulfilled a role as a market for the goods that were bought in China and Southeast Asia.

Trade with Japan was conducted on an official level by sending missions to the Muromachi Shogunate as well as privately through merchant transactions in Sakai, Hakata, and Tsushima. The Ryukyuan merchants brought Chinese raw silk, silk fabrics and ceramics and wares from Southeast Asia including spices and medicines to Japan which they traded for Japanese produced craft items such as swords, lacquer ware and fans. The goods brought by the Ryukyuan traders were considered priceless by the upper classes of the Muromachi Shogunate and the trade was warmly welcomed.

By the middle of the 15th century the Muromachi Shogunate was becoming weaker, there were civil disturbances and pirates appeared more frequently so the trading ships heading toward Japan decreased. On the other hand the merchant ships from Japan came to call more frequently in the Ryukyus and trade was conducted there.

Establishment of the Ryukyu Kingdom

The Second Sho Dynasty

After the reign of Sho Hashi, who united the Ryukyus and established the First Sho Dynasty, the power of the royal court began to taper off. The 7th king to assume the throne in the Ryukyus was Sho Toku who was ambitious in his pursuit of territorial expansion. Without regard to incidents of civil strife and worsening financial conditions from shrine and temple building projects, his reign grew increasingly tyrannical.

After his death by illness, the powerful vassals at court met and recommended that the chief vassal Kanemaru assume the throne. Kanemaru was born in a farming household but his genius was recognized by the 6th heir to the throne King Sho Taikyu and he was appointed to handle foreign diplomacy and finances for the court. Kanemaru took office using the name Sho En, with the Sho part of his name borrowed from the names of the First Sho Dynasty kings. King Sho En informed the Chinese emperor of the succession and received investiture envoys from China in 1472. His reign began what is called the Second Sho Dynasty which continued unbroken over 19 generations of kings, for 410 years, until the "Disposition of the Ryukyus" edict issued by the Japanese government in the early Meiji era (1868 - 1912).

Genealogy of the Second Sho Dynasty (Early period)

King	Period of Reign	Number of Years
Sho En	1470 - 1476	7 years
Sho Seni	1477	1 years
Sho Shin	1477 - 1526	50 years
Sho Sei	1527 - 1555	29 years
Sho Gen	1556 - 1572	17 years
Sho Ei	1573 - 1588	16 years
Sho Nei	1589 - 1620	32 years

The Government of King Sho Shin

The 3rd successor to the throne of the Second Sho Dynasty was Sho Shin. His reign left behind some of the most exceptional achievements of the dynasty. He was king during what is called the Golden Age of the Ryukyu Kingdom.

After the death of King Sho En, the king's brother succeeded him but abdicated after a reign of less than 6 months after which Sho Shin became king at the young age of 12. During Sho Shin's long 50-year reign he was gradually able to build up a centralized government with the king in power.

One of the first reforms he carried out was requiring the local regional chieftains, known as Aji, to reside in the capital Shuri and set up a political bureaucracy to manage rule over the regions. Furthermore, he ordered the establishment of a class system that could be instantly recognizable by the color and materials of the hats (Hachimachi) and ornamental hairpins (Kanzashi) worn by the Aji.

Sho Shin also partitioned the islands, municipalities, and sections of the villages and towns into the jurisdictions currently in use in Okinawa. The sphere of the administration also included the Amami and Miyako Islands.

Sho Shin's reign also saw the systematization of the priestesses (Noro) with a supreme high priestess called the Kikoe Ogimi. This system was intended to exercise a spiritual control over the power of the court.

With the financial resources gained through intermediary trading, Sho Shin instituted many engineering projects throughout the kingdom.

All of these accomplishments helped to establish a centralized state and a period with a prosperity that can be appropriately called "The Golden Age of the

Construction and Cultural Enterprises

The centralized power of the governmental system under King Sho Shin instituted many construction and cultural projects at Shurijo Castle.

Starting in 1492 with the construction of the royal family temple Bodaiji located within Enkakuji Temple, the series of building projects carried out under his rule include Hojo-kyo Bridge, Enkanchi Pond, The stone gate Sunuhyan-Utaki Ishimon , Benke-Utaki Shrine. Tamaudun Royal Mausoleum, and other projects.

An important road connecting Shurijo Castle with the southern parts of the kingdom, the Madamichi road and the Madanbashi Bridge were also constructed.

A major cultural achievement in his reign was the beginning of compilation of the Omoro-soushi. The Omoro are ancient ballads and songs handed down on the Okinawa and Amami Islands. These were transcribed and edited to become the Omoro-soushi, a major literary work of the Ryukyus.

Rivalry of the Sakishima Warlords

Around the beginning of the 14th century, when the Aji regional chieftains were struggling with each other for power on the main island of Okinawa, the outlying Sakishima Islands (Sakishima Island and the Miyako and Yaeyama Islands) began to develop agrarian villages in each of their regions. The village chiefs, called by various titles such as Tenta, Azu, and Kaara started to vie with each other for supremacy in struggles in a period termed the Age of the Rival Warlords or Gunyukakkyo.

On Miyako during the mid 14th century chieftains fought each other over who was to rule and the state of affairs deteriorated into confusion. The strongest of these warlords, named Meguro-muitui-miya, succeeded in unifying the island. However another powerful Aji, Yonaha-dutui-miya, pleged allegiance to King Satto on the main island of Okinawa in hopes of increasing his power. The result was that Miyako was divided into two powers.

In the middle part of the 15th century Meguro-muitui-miya's successor Nakasone-tuimiya, noted for his distinguished leadership, was appointed leader of the whole island of Miyako-jima in 1474 by King Sho En.

As Miyako-jima was unified, the neighboring Yaeyama Islands were engaged in violent struggles for hegemony even as they traded with each other.

Also, on islands such as Yonaguni and Iriomote, which were somewhat under the control of Miyako-jima Island, there was resistance to being controlled by either Miyako or Yaeyama. Finally, there was the Ryukyu Court which sought to rule them all. It was a period when complex military confrontations came to the surface

Oyake-Akahachi Rebellion

In the latter 15th century on the Sakishima Islands (Sakishima Island, and the Miyako and Yaeyama Islands) there were violent confrontations between the leader of Miyako, Nakasone-tuimiya, who was appointed by the Ryukyuan King Sho En, and the as yet un-unified Aji regional chieftains of Yaeyama Island.

Within Yaeyama, there was rivalry between the powerful warlord Oyake-Akahachi and Nata-Ufushu. Rebellion broke out when Nata-

Ufushu, who was a vassal of the Rykyuan King Sho En , allied himself with Nakasone- Tuimiya of Miyako in order to unify the island. Oyake-Akahachi rebelled and attempted to form an independent Yaeyama. The Oyake-Akahachi Rebellion was recorded by the Ryukyuan Royal Government in the history "Kyuyo" as follows.

A man named Oyake- Akahachi Hon-gawara from the Ohama region of Yaeyama, without giving allegiance nor tribute, sought to rebel and held ambitions to rule both the Yaeyama and Miyako islands. The Royal Government dispatched an expeditionary force and together with Miyako's Nakasone-Tuimiya and Shitabaru Ojiru left for Ishigaki-jima Island. Meeting the defenses of the battle-prepared Akahachi forces, the King's army found it difficult to make a landing on the island. However due to an ingenious strategy employed the Noro Chinpe (a priestess) the landing was at last successful and the King's forces swept over the enemy in one strike, crushing the ambitions of Oyake-Akahachi.

As reward for their victory in war, the King ordered that Nakasone-Tuimiya be given leadership over Miyako-jima Island and his second son, Machirigani-Tuimiya be given leadership over Yaeyama with the title Kashirashoku. This was the first time that the royal court posted a leader to govern the Sakishima Islands.

Through this the grasp the Ryukyuan Royal Government had on the Sakishima islands was strengthened to yet another level. Furthermore, after the Onitora Revolt on Yonaguni Island was put down, the court was able to gain complete rule over the Sakishima Islands.

The Later Period Ryukyu

The great age of trade, which was established by the Ryukyu Kingdom throughout East Asia, ended with the appearance of the Western European powers in the 16th century. The amicable trade relationship which had been built with Japan began to show changes. The Shimazu Clan of Satsuma began to approach the Ryukyus with territorial ambitions, eventually culminating in a Satsuma invasion of the Ryukyu Kingdom with a Shogunate sponsored military force in 1609. The Ryukyu Kingdom, weak militarily and having virtually no experience in battle after long peaceful years as a kingdom, was subordinated, without any real resistance, under the Satsuma clan.

The Shimazu invasion did not result in the dismantlement of the Ryukyu Kingdom, and its hegemony by Satsuma was concealed from China. Satsuma imposed taxes to be paid in rice and other commodities. The lucrative trade and many other facets of life were controlled by their rules. The Ryukyus were also required to send processions to Edo (Tokyo) to pay obeisance to the Shogunate.

Within this age of disorder, the Ryukyus were fortunate to have had the appearance of bold and able reform leaders such as Choshu Haneji and Saion. Facing up to the reality of Satsuma domination, they tried to save the Ryukyu Kingdom through policies based on cooperation with the Satsuma clan. It was time that the traditional political system of the Ancient Ryukyus ended and the road to a new modern age in the Ryukyu Kingdom opened up.

The Latter Period Ryukyus was an age of even more advancement and development. The kingdom actively absorbed culture from Japan and China. Harmonizing the diverse cultural influences from Japan and China developed most of the Ryukyuan culture's rich distinctiveness. The traditional Okinawan culture we enjoy today was cultivated in this early modern age.

Shimazu Invasion of the Ryukyus

Relations between Toyotomi Hideyoshi, the Shimazu Clan and the Ryukyu Kingdom

The Age of Great Trade for the Ryukyu Kingdom came to an end in the 16th century; however, trade with China still remained active. It became economically vital for the Shimazu to allow the Ryukyu Kingdom to continue to exist in name as an independent nation.

During this period in Japan, Toyotomi Hideyoshi (one of Japan's three greatest military leaders) unified the whole country and issued an edict requiring other areas of Japan to pay a portion of the military burden. This edict was extended to the then independent nation of the Ryukyu Kingdom via the Shimazu Clan of Satsuma. The demand combined the military burden of the Ryukyus with Satsuma and included the dispatch of an army of 15,000 troops. However, since the Ryukyu Kingdom had no experience in battle, it was exempted from the demand for the troop dispatch and instead was to deliver provisions of rice for 7,000 troops for a period of ten months.

Coinciding with this development was the enthronement of a new king in the Ryukyus, King Sho Nei. This increased the economic difficulty of the kingdom due to the requirement they had to welcome the Chinese investiture envoys. The suzerain relationship the Ryukyu Kingdom had with Ming China had been the most important relation for them. The Ryukyu worried that if they acceded to the Japanese demands it would negatively affect their relations with China. They heatedly debated this within the court. Finally, fearful of an impending attack from the Shimazu should the demands be rejected, they agreed to pay half the amount of the military burden.

The Shimazu Invasion

The dispatch of troops to Korea was ended with the death of Toyotomi Hideyoshi in 1598. Tokugawa Ieyasu, who held most of the power in Japan, requested mediation from the Ryukyu Kingdom in order to restore the relationship with China, which had become strained due to the dispatch of troops to Korea. At the same time they hoped to get the Ryukyus under the control of the Shogunate. The Ryukyu Kingdom regarded relations with Ming as a priority and did not accede to the demands of the Shogunate. The Shimazu clan was in charge of negotiations to get the Ryukyus to obey the demands and also saw it as a chance to extricate itself from it's own financial difficulties.

The Shimazu initiated planning to invade the Ryukyus. Initially the Shogunate refrained from military force, however unable to endure the obstinate refusal from Ryukyus; it issued the order allowing the Shimazu clan to carry out their invasion plan of the Ryukyus. The Shimazu clan entered the Ryukyu Islands through Amami Oshima Island and attacked with a force of some 3,000 in March 1609. The Ryukyu Kingdom having neither the weapons nor experience to do battle was defeated with minimal resistance in only ten days and was forced under Satsuma hegemony. King Sho Nei and his ministers were taken captive to Satsuma and detained for about two years. King Sho Nei underwent humiliation and was coerced into a written oath that stated; "Neither I, King Sho Nei, nor my descendents will ever betray the Shimazu clan." Though the Ryukyu Kingdom was still claimed to be an independent country, it was in fact subordinated under the Tokugawa.

Shimazu Hegemony

Establishing the Kingdom of the Ryukyus

In establishing the Shimazu clan's rule over the Kingdom of the Ryukyus, the invaders first surveyed land and imposed the obligation to pay land tax in rice. They forced King Sho Nei and his Sanshikan (high officials who took charge of state affairs and assisted the king) to submit a written pledge which promised loyalty to the Shimazu Clan. The contents of this written pledge were as follows:

"The Ryukyu Kingdom was subjugated by the Satsuma clan because of neglect of duty to the Shogunate and Shimazu Clan. Therefore, the Ryukyus were crushed once, however through the generosity of the Shimazu, the Okinawa Islands, except Amami-jima Island, are given back again. We will not forget this grace in the generations of descendants to come and will never betray the Shimazu clan."

One of the Sanshikan, Jahana Ekata, continued to refuse the unilateral nature of the pledge and was executed by Satsuma. The Shimazu Clan sent local magistrates in order to keep the Ryukyu Kingdom under observation as well as established "The Fifteen Articles" under which the Ryukyu Kingdom was controlled by the Shimazu clan.

Jana Ekata Teido

Jana Ekata Teido was one of the upper level ministers, or Sanshikan, who assisted the Ryukyuan king. After the Shimazu invasion, when he was taken to Satsuma with King Sho Nei, the Shimazu attempted to force Jana to write a pledge promising loyalty to the Shimazu clan. However, as he felt entrusted with the government, he refused all the serial demands rationalizing the invasion by the Shimazu and resisted Satsuma domain to the end. Jana tried a secret escape to a Chinese boat, which was visiting Nagasaki shore and hoped he would receive help from Ming China. But it ended in failure and as a result the Shimazu decapitated him in 1611. China reported Jana as a "loyal retainer who sacrificed himself in time of national crisis".

The Fifteen Articles

The Fifteen Articles or rules, which became the framework for Shimazu hegemony over the Ryukyu Kingdom were established and promulgated in 1611. The contents were as follows:

1. There will be no goods ordered from Tang (China) without the command from the Satsuma clan.

2. No land will be bequeathed any persons who are not currently government officials.

3. No land or government duties are to be bestowed on women.

4. No personal male servants are to employed by individuals.

5. No building an excessive number of Buddhist temples or Shinto shrines.

6. Satsuma approval is required of merchants.

7. There is to be no purchase and transport of Ryukyuans to Japan.

8. The Ryukyus must deliver land taxes and other public property as established by the Satsuma magistrates.

9. The office of Sanshikan is not to be ignored or bypassed.

10. There are to be no coerced sales or purchases.

11. Quarreling is prohibited.

12. Small crimes shall be dealt with through the offices of the Chonin-hyakucho (low-level village officials) but the greater ones shall be referred to Satsuma.

13. Ryukyu must not dispatch trade ships to other territories.

14. Only Japanese measures are to be used.

15. Gambling and other immoral activities are prohibited.

A "Foreign Country" within Japan

Trade with China needed to be maintained because of the economic ambitions of Shimazu and the Ryukyuan desire for the continuation of the Kingdom of the Ryukyus. The kingdom had the obligation to dispatch emissaries on visits to Edo (Tokyo) on occasions such as the enthronement of a new king of the Ryukyus and the assumption of power of a new Shogun. This was seen as an expression of subordination and courtesy to the Shogunate and Satsuma clan. The journey of these processions were called " Edo nobori" or procession to Edo (Tokyo). The Shogunate and Shimazu clan used these occasions to ostentatiously display their power to rule over another foreign country and were seen by both the Shogunate and Shimazu as a chance to increase their authority.

Tributary Trade Under Shimazu Hegemony

In the 17th century, after the Shimazu invasion, the government of China also changed from the Ming Dynasty to the Ching Dynasty. Despite this, trade with the Ryukyu Kingdom continued. The tribute and trading vassals rode on ships sailing toward China. Tens of them proceeded to Beijing and the remainder at Ryukyuan Hall in Fukien to perform business transactions with Chinese merchants. When the Ukanshin Crown ships arrived in the Ryukyus for investiture ceremonies there were also several hundred merchants and many trading goods accompanying the Sappushi envoys. The government of the Ryukyu Kingdom needed to purchase these products at appropriate prices.

The Ryukyu Kingdom's finances during those days were provided for by a monopoly on trade goods such as sugar and turmeric. However, due to the land taxes extracted by the Shimazu Clan, the Ryukyu government had to borrow more than half of the funds needed to trade with China from Shimazu or the merchants of Satsuma Domain. The financial pressure on them was very severe. In return for this the merchants were given discounted prices and priority when purchasing Ryukyuan sugar.

When the merchants of Satsuma collected the trading products to bring into China in Kyoto or Osaka, they borrowed silver from business houses in Kyoto or Osaka and supplied funds for the Ryukyuan trade with China. In this way the Ryukyu government of those days maintained tribute and trade relations with China by depending on Shimazu clan or Satsuma merchants. As a result, the Chinese products, which were brought in, were handed over to Shimazu or Satsuma merchants as payment for the silver lent to the Ryukyuans to buy the trade goods. Both the Shimazu Clan and Satsuma Domain took advantage of tribute and trade relations between Ryukyu and China to receive lucrative profits.

Kelp and Okinawa

Since Zuiken Kawamura (1617-1699) discovered the westward and eastern sailing routes in the middle of 17th century, large quantities of marine products from the land of the Ainu people (Hokkaido) was carried to Edo (Tokyo)and Osaka. At the end of 18th century, Satsuma merchants exchanged kelp, which was transported to Osaka from Hokkaido through the Japan Sea, for sugar. They also took advantage of Ryukyu's tribute and trading with China and to export kelp to China. And they purchased materials such as raw silk, fabrics and Chinese medicine from China in exchange.

Kelp occupied 70-90 % of the freight from Ryukyu to China after the 1820's. This was about 10 % of the gross weight produced in Japan. Even an office of the "Kelp Magistrate" was established in Naha in the middle of 19th century. Kelp was a very important export product for the Ryukyu Kingdom until tribute and trading with China was severed by dissolution of the kingdom. Kelp became not only an export product but also largely influenced to the cuisine of the Ryukyuan people. It became a quintessential part of their diet, as is pork. Even today the per capita consumption of kelp is the greatest in Japan. Okinawans credit kelp with helping to make them as long-lived as they are.

Reconstruction of the Ryukyu Kingdom

Reforms of Haneji Choshu

After the Shimazu invasion in 1609, despite the passing of half a century, the Ryukyu Kingdom was still in a state of confusion. People had lost their vigor. During this period of confusion, it was Haneji Choshu who began to strike bold political reform and began the reconstruction of the Ryukyu Kingdom. He aided in the conversion of Ryukyuan society from the Ancient Ryukyus to the Latter Period Ryukyus. He also has a Chinese name, Sho Jo ken. When he became Regent (minister who assists king and takes charge in state affairs) he made the following reforms:

1. The prohibition of luxury for all classes including the royal families to encourage thrift.

2. The prohibition of prostitution and strict enforcement of moral discipline.

3. Elimination of the political influence of the supreme priestess and other court ladies and reform in the customs of traditional religion.

4. Controls on the unjust practices of public officials and promotion of land reclamation by farmers in order to reconstruct devastated agricultural villages.

5. Allowed the samurai to learn the cultural accomplishments of the Ryukyus and persuaded them of the necessity for education as a tool in the negotiations with the Satsuma Domain.

These various precepts were organized and called the Haneji Shioki (Haneji Chastisements).

The Ideas of Haneji Choshu

The bold political reform which Haneji Choshu performed was within the context of a theory called "Nichi Ryu Doso Ron " which stipulated that the ancestry of the Ryukyuan people and the Japanese were originally the same. In order to establish cooperative relations with Satsuma Domain, the rule of the Ryukyus by Satsuma needed to be rationalized under the basis of such theories as this. Haneji edited the "Chuzan Sei Kan", the official history of the Ryukyus Kingdom on the basis of the Nichi Ryu Doso Ron theory before he became regent. This is the first official history of the Ryukyus. It wrote that the Ryukyus had relations with Japan from ancient times as historical fact. Haneji's realistic policy was promoted as a reform to lead the confused kingdom to reconstruction and took on an important role in allowing the Ryukyu Kingdom to change with the times. Through his reforms the kingdom underwent a period of internal criticism.

Construction of the Administrative Structure

The pre-existing administrative structure was reorganized by the political reforms of Haneji Choshu. The nucleus of the Ryukyu Kingdom's government was called "Hyo-Jo-Sho" and was divided into the Sanshikan ministers; Regencies, Magistrates and civil officials called Moushi Kuchi Ho. The Hyo-Jo-Sho was the supreme authority and was in charge of making decisions on matters within the kingdom. It was divided into an organization called the Uinu Uza which was administered by the regency and Sanshikan ministers and the Shimunza which consisted of 15 public officials of the Mono Bugyo and Moushi Kuchi Ho.

All important issues were discussed and the recommendations were conveyed to the King for final decision. While the chief and a vice-chiefs of the Mono Bugyo and Moushi Kuchi Ho were members of Hyo-Jo-Sho, they took charge of the direct administration. Financial affairs were conducted under the jurisdiction of four administrative sections called the Sasunu Suba, the Soushikuri, the Tomari Jito, and the Hira-jo established under the Mono Bugyo. Jurisdiction for diplomacy and the domestic administration came under three agencies, the Shotaiho, the Kyuchi-kata and the Yoi kata that were established under the Moushi Kuchi Ho.

Establishment of the Class System

The original form of the class system of the Ryukyu Kingdom was created in the reign of King Sho Shin at the end of the 15th century over into the 16th century. In the 17th century the people were divided into three classes, the Daimyo, Samurai, and farmers. Distinctions between Samurai and farmer were made very clear by compilation of the Kafu; a genealogical table worked out by Choshu Haneji starting around 1670. Samurai were ordered to make genealogical tables and were then classified as "Kei mochi" which means those having a genealogy. Farmers, having no genealogy table were classified as "Mukei" meaning those who were without. Social status was clarified by the existence of genealogical table. Descendants of the samurai rank were divided into two classes called Daimyo and Samurai.

The princes, Aji chieftains, and Ekata belonged to the Daimyo category. Those of the Daimyo rank were the highest rulers and they were given an area of jurisdiction called a "Magiri" corresponding to a modern city or village. Large residences where princes and Aji chieftains lived were called Udun and residences for Ekata class were called Dunchi. Samurai who came from major Daimyo families were called Satunushi-sujime and were engaged in important posts befitting higher-class samurai descendants. The remaining samurai were called Chikudun-sujime and engaged in general administrative work as a lower class samurai. Chikudun-sujime included farmers who became samurai by meritorious deeds or contributions even though they did not originally have a genealogical table. On the other hand, farmers were divided into town farmers who lived around the Naha and Shuri area and engaged in commerce and industry and the countryside farmers who lived in the country and dealt strictly in agriculture.

The Reforms of Saion

Saion was another reformer who continued much the same work and ideology of Haneji Choshu and helped bring about important political reform by advancing various polices. Saion was from Kumemura, a place where many of the Chinese stayed when in the Ryukyus. He studied Confucianism and divination (Fusui) from a young age and went to China to be schooled in the practical sciences to aid in the reconstruction of the Ryukyu Kingdom. Saion's talent did not escape the court and he achieved the high rank of Sanshikan in 1728. His policies were similar to Haneji's in his belief of the importance of cooperative policies toward the Satsuma domain that ruled them. He attempted to secure forest resources, achieve financial reconstruction of the Ryukyu Kingdom, including revitalization of the agricultural villages, which were suffering from abject poverty.

Saion first established life improvement precepts called the Go-kyo-jo based on Confucian thought in order to secure greater control over the agricultural villages. And he preached that all people, including farmers and public officials should follow its moral precepts. Movement from the agricultural areas to the city was prohibited under agricultural policies. Farmers were urged to concentrate on improvements in agricultural production.

Saion himself journeyed throughout the island to promoted river improvements and irrigation. Reforestation and other forest conservation policies were one of the valued achievements of Saion. An increase in population at that time caused increased consumption of resources such as construction materials and firewood. Saion appraised the situation and established regulations for replanting and taught forest management methods.

In financial reconstruction of the government of Ryukyu Kingdom, he strengthened the Ryukyu monopoly system for the important trade goods turmeric and crude sugar, which were special products of from the Ryukyus. Furthermore, a system was created to purchase raw sugar at a low price outside of the tax. There was naturally much criticism in this kind of powerful political reform. A scholar, Heshikiya Chobin, who was subsequently executed as a rebel, started one incident of resistance to the new policies of the government of the Ryukyu Kingdom. While Saion carried out the administration of the kingdom, he also wrote many books utilizing his various academic experiences. These writings influenced the bureaucracies of the early modern age. Scholars such as Iha Fuyu and Majikina Anko in modern Okinawa conducted study of his works as well

Conditions in Rural Agricultural Villages

In the Latter Period Ryukyus, families of the samurai class and town farmers lived in the urban districts, and farmers lived in the countryside. Movement of residence was strictly prohibited. There were some exceptions to this rule, such as when it was permitted for a Samurai to engage in agriculture in cases where there was no work and they immigrated into an agricultural area. The villages of samurai like this were called Yadoi. In the ancient Ryukyus, the municipalities were called Magiri and Shima. The Magiri became modern cities or towns, the designation Shima corresponds to the current designation of village. In the Latter Period Ryukyus, public offices called Bandokoro and Muraya were established to replace the Magiri and Shima system. A farmer with leadership qualities was appointed as Jito, a kind of feudal lord and a total of five officials were charged with administrating a Bandokoro office. Additionally, lower ranked public officials were placed in charge of administration and guidance of cultivated and timbered land.

These were placed in city offices called Muraya. Within the cultivated area of an agricultural village, land was provided to farmers for agriculture, and also to the Jito, Magiri public officials, and ceremonial priestesses called Noro. Other areas that were not yet in cultivation were approved for reclamation as private land. Farmers had a duty to pay land tax in rice or sugar as well as cultivate the land of the officials of the villages. They had to pay two-thirds of their income to the Ryukyu Kingdom, Jito, district public officials and Noro priestesses, obtaining one third of their production as profit. The weight of this tax duty was an extreme burden to the farmers. This, together with strict enforcement in levying land tax caused a contradictory increase in nonpayment and the impoverishment of agricultural villages.

The Devastation in the Agricultural Villages

In the 18th century agricultural villages suffering from exploitive land taxes became increasingly devastated. This was aggravated by the recurrent natural disasters that hit the Ryukyus, such as typhoons and droughts. In agricultural villages a poverty gap occurred between the rich farmer class and the poor farmer class. The poor farmer could not help giving members of his family away, practicing infanticide or selling out a member for a contracted term of labor. There were farmers who could not pay taxes and failed individually as well as entire groups of farmers who were unable to pay within the group units they were organized into.

The staple food of farmers in those days was sweet potatoes. However, even production of sweet potatoes, which have a short crop cycle and are resistant to natural disasters, fell and were sometimes not stockpiled in large enough supply. This caused many people to die of starvation. During these times of starvation, the local Sotetsu Cycads (Cycas revoluta Thunb.) were used for food. The Cycad is a poisonous plant related to the palm family. If processing methods are faulty, consumption can cause death. Food shortages in those days were very serious. The government of the Ryukyu Kingdom encouraged cultivation of cycad while giving guidance on methods for handling the toxins. The kingdom dispatched public officials to reconstruct the devastated agricultural villages, however the reality of agricultural village life was grim. Even the reformers had difficulty dealing with the poverty. This meant fiscal failure of for the government of the Ryukyu Kingdom as the economy was based on agriculture. Famine and epidemic prevailed in the Ryukyus during this period.

The Conditions of Rule in the Sakishima Islands

The Sakishima Islands (the Miyako-jima and Yaeyama Island groups) began to be ruled by the government of the Ryukyu Kingdom after the revolt of Oyake Akahachi in 1500. Rule over the islands in those days was still indirect. With de facto rule over the Ryukyu Kingdom by the Satsuma Domain after 1609, the government of the Ryukyu Kingdom had to further strengthen its hold over the Sakishima islands. To accomplish this a Ryukyu Kingdom government branch office called the Kuramoto was established and public officials called Zeban were dispatched from the capital of Shuri. The land surveying by Satsuma included the mainland of Okinawa and extended to the Sakishima Islands. The results became the basis for the amount of tribute handed over to Satsuma. The government of the Ryukyu Kingdom established a per capita tax system on the Sakishima Islands. This method imposes a per head tax without considering the area of field cultivation. Once population increased and cultivated area was enlarged, productivity seemed to rise as well with this system. However, disasters such as the Meiwa Tsunami in the late of 18th century occurred and productivity decreased with the deaths in the population. Even in these situations, the government continued to impose taxes strictly, and the agricultural villages of Sakishima Island became even further impoverished.

Per Capita Taxation

The per capita tax was imposed on each man and woman from ages of fifteen to fifty. It was levied without considering the area of the fields that were cultivated. Generally this taxation system is said to have been a great burden in the historical writings. In actual fact the per capita had been performing well in the Sakishima Islands (the Miyako-jima and Yaeyama islands). Initially the tax rate was not very high. The reason why it had such a bad reputation was that people had other taxes called Tokoro-zukai-mai imposed in addition to this, leading to exploitation by public officials. The people suffered greatly from the dishonesty of local public officials.

The Meiwa Tsunami

The gigantic Meiwa Tsunami which brought serious damage to the Miyako-jima and Yaeyama Islands started as the eruption of an undersea volcano, causing an earthquake in the southeastern area of the seas off Ishigaki-jima Island in April of 1771. The tsunami hit the seashore of southeastern of Ishigaki-jima Island. The initial part of tidal wave peaked at a spot 84.5 meters above sea level. Damage amounted to the destruction of 2,176 houses and 2,223 rice bales were flushed away. Deaths amounted to 9,313 people; one third of Yaeyama's total population was lost. After the tsunami, other natural disasters and epidemics broke out. It was said that the spread of epidemic was mostly a man-made disaster.

When post-tsunami epidemics broke in the same year as the Meiwa tsunami in the southern part of mainland Okinawa, grain was provided to those afflicted. However, in the case of the Yaeyama tsunami, people were not provided with any food and damage grew even greater than before because of deaths by starvation. In addition, the government levied the amount of the per capita tax on those dead who had not paid. It meant that people who survived were coerced into forced labor to redeem their debt. The population of Yaeyama continued to decrease because of other natural disasters, epidemics and taxation. It had decreased to one third of the population before the tsunami in the latter part of the Ryukyu Kingdom.

The tsunami brought severe damage to Miyakojima-island as well. It is written in Miyako historical records that 2,548 people died. The tsunami surged up to 30 meters above sea level.

The Flourishing Industry and Culture of the Latter Period Ryukyus

Agricultural Developments

The sweet potato is said to be one of the most typical Okinawan agricultural products. It is believed that Noguni Sokan brought it back to the Ryukyus from China in 1605 and his lord, Gima Shinjo, studied the methods of cultivation and spread it throughout the Ryukyus. The Ryukyu Archipelago is known for frequently suffering through famines brought on by natural disasters such as typhoons. The advent of a crop like the sweet potato was revolutionary in the Ryukyus because of its ability to withstand the changeable climate. Later the sweet potato spread from the Ryukyus to Satsuma and was introduced to the whole of Japan by Aoki Konyo. In Japanese it is called the Satsuma-Imo or Satsuma potato and was named after the domain in southern Kyushu.

Another one of the typical Okinawan farm products is sugar cane. The time at which the Satsuma-Imo was imported from Ryukyu is unknown, however it is believed that Gima Shinjo, who introduced the sweet potato, dispatched retainers to China to learn sugar manufacturing methods in 1623. The government of the Ryukyu Kingdom soon realized that sugar cane could be traded at a high price in Japan, similar to the profits the Ryukyus received by its monopoly on sales of turmeric. A sugar magistrate was established in 1662 to exercise control over cultivation and sugar manufacture

Arts and Crafts Development

Artisans skilled in the various arts and crafts were employed by the government of the Ryukyu Kingdom and emigrated to Shuri or Naha in the 17th century. Arts and crafts were developed to meet the wholesale as well as private market demands. Arts and crafts were actively encouraged for the samurais who did not have professions as part of the policies of reconstruction developed by Saion in 1728. Crafts such as metalworking in gold, silver, and copper, textiles, such as dyed cloth, liquor making, miso and soy sauce manufacture, cabinet-working, sculpture, lacquerware and wood crafts were developed in Shuri.

Construction of Transportation Networks

Under Japanese rule the Ryukyu Kingdom established signal fires which were in important strategic positions and quickly transmitted information on the arrival of foreign ships. On the Sakishima Islands (the Miyakojima and Yaeyama Island groups) fast ships were equipped for urgent communications with the government as well. Domestic transportation networks were formed around Naha, the trading center for provisions as well as the major port of the Ryukyus. Inns to stay at were called Magiri Yado, Shima Yado, or Mura Yado and were often crowded with people because public officials frequently came over to Shuri and Naha on official business. A main road connecting the jurisdictions was called the Shuku Michi (Inn road). Administrative orders were conveyed along this road to each district from the government of the kingdom. The roads of throughout the Ryukyu kingdom developed and spread around this Shuku Michi.

The culture in latter period of Ryukyus

The political and economic pressure of the Shimazu invasion stressed the culture of the latter period Ryukyus. However, in this new environment the Ryukyuans actively absorbed Japanese culture and harmonized it with their own. Through this process a new and original Ryukyuan culture emerged at the dawn of the early modern age. In particular, the reign of the 18th century of King Sho Kei has been called the "Golden Age of Ryukyuan Culture". Most of the Okinawan traditional culture transmitted down to the present time was cultivated during this period. However, the central cultural figures of culture of the time were mainly of samurai or aristocrat descent. It was not culture created by the common folk. This brilliant culture, created in the latter period Ryukyus, is therefore often referred to as dynastic or courts culture.

Culture of the Latter Ryukyu Kingdom
(Compilation of Official Histories and Establishment of the Legal System.)

The Chuzan Sekan: The First Official History

The "Chuzan Sekan" was the first official history and was edited by Haneji Choshu in 1650. This historical record was based on the Nichiryu Doso Ron ideology that states that the Japanese and Ryukyuan people were originally of the same race. The political purpose of this was to raise the awareness of Ryukyuans after the advent of Shimazu rule.

The "Chuzan Seifu"

The Chuzan Seifu was the classical Chinese translation of the Chuzan Sekan by done first Saitaku in 1701 and was revised by Saion in 1726. However, the relations between the Ryukyu Kingdom and Satsuma were contained in a separate volume so that China would not know of the dual tribute relations of the Ryukyus.

The "Ryukyu Koku Yurai Ki"

(Record of the Origins of the Ryukyu Kingdom).

This set of 21 volumes is the oldest topographic description of the islands and was edited by government of the Ryukyu Kingdom in 1713. It contains the ceremonial events of the castles, old chronicles and the origin of each place, sacred Utaki and even includes the government official system of the royal castle. This is a very important document for understanding traditional Ryukyuan society.

The "Kyuyo"

This book is an official history which Tei-hei-tetsu was ordered to complete by the government in 1745. An original volume contained a record of the events that took place in each region of the Ryukyus. An attached volume contained a record of relations between Ryukyu and Satsuma. Another volume contained a collection of legends and old tales collected from various places in Ryukyus.

The "Ryukyu Karitsu"

A book of laws for the Ryukyus written with reference to the laws of Japan and China. This was written in Japanese in 1786. In 1831, a new series of was edited as additional laws were enacted. In 1860, the government had the articles of the laws that were promulgated, recited to give the common folk some understanding of the law and for the purpose of crime prevention

Latter Period Ryukyuan Developments in Academics and Literature

Ryukyuan academics and literature were influenced by both of Japan and China. However, the language came from Japanese roots and classical Chinese was read in the Japanese way.

The "Rikuyu Engi"

This is a book on morality which Teijunsoku, also known as Nago Ekata Chobun, brought back from China to the Ryukyus when he was young. Later it was sent through Satsuma to the Shogunate and was translated into Japanese by Ogyu Sorai and Muro Kyusou. It spread throughout the whole country as a textbook in the Teragoya temple schools of the Edo Period.

"Konkou Kenshu"

A dictionary of the archaic Rykyuan language completed in 1711. It is believed that Shikina Seimei was the planner of the dictionary. There are quotations from Japanese literature such as the "Genji Monogatari" (Tale of the Genji), "Ise Monogatari" (Tales of Ise) and the "Tsurezure-gusa" (Essays in Idleness) throughout the book. At the time, most literature scholars in the Ryukyus were proficient in the

Japanese style Waka. Poem gatherings were held at the daimyo's residence in Shuri every month. The king was also in attendance at some of these gatherings.

Ryuka (Okinawan Lyrical poetry)

The Ryuka is a significant genre in classical Okinawan literature. A short poem form, the Ryuka contains four lines of 8-8-8-6 syllables and expresses a spontaneous emotion. 8 and 6 syllables were characteristic of verse in the Ryukyus since the days of the Manyo-shu (Nara period). Ryuka flourished under the stimulating influence of Waka and the musical accompaniment of the Sanshin (Okinawan samisen) which was introduced from China in the late of 14th century. There are songs that are still popular today such as those of the women poets, Unna Nabi and Yoshiya Umichiru, both of whom wove skilled and delicate verses.

Kumi-odori Dance

The Ryukyuan classical theater Kumi-odori was created for entertainments presented to welcome Chinese investiture envoys. It is a unique Ryukyuan genre in theater, which combines music, dancing and verse. Kumi-odori was created by Tamagusuku Chokun (1684-1734) and was first performed at the ceremonies for Chinese investiture envoys held in 1719. The plots are taken from tales and legends transmitted orally for generations, however its style and direction were influenced by the Japanese classical theater arts of Noh, Puppet theater, and Kabuki. There are five masterpieces that are considered Tamagusuku Chokun's finest work. Nido Tekiuchi" (Revenge of the Two Boys), "Shushin Kaneiri "(Passion and the Bell), "Mekarushi" (Master Mekaru), "Unna-munu-gurui" (The Madwoman) and "Koko no Makai" (Filial Piety). Another well-known and popular work is that of Heshikiya Chobin (1700-1734) who wrote "Temizu no En" (A Handful of Water).

Ryukyuan Culture in the Latter Period Ryukyus
The Establishment of Schools

The educational system in the Ryukyus began with the dispatch students to the Kokushikan in China around 1392. Higher education usually meant travel to China. Teijunsoku established the Meirin-Do School in Kume village in 1718 and began practical diplomatic and bureaucratic training for students including the language of Beijing, Confucianism and the drafting of diplomatic documents. In 1798 Hira Gakko public schools were established and the study of ancient Japanese thought and culture was established into the upper level schools. These schools became training institutes for high government officials. Local village schools were established in each village by 1846.

However, the only students who were allowed to study there were children of samurai descendents. Other schools for the practice of writing and calculation were established for the children of district officials

Culture of the Latter Period Ryukyus
Calligraphy, Tea ceremony, Music, and Dance
Calligraphy

Of the famous calligraphers of the period, three are outstanding, Sonnen Gusukuma of the Oie school of calligraphy in the 17th century, as well as Teishu and Teikakun who were famous as calligraphers and studied in China in the late 16th century.

Tea ceremony

Zen priests introduced the Tea ceremony in the early 17th century. The Buddhist priest, Sakai was appointed master of tea ceremony and this art spread through the upper class. The Tea ceremony was performed to entertain foreign diplomats. A teahouse, Ochaya Udun, was built in the Sakiyama area of Shuri during the reign of King Sho Tei. Ryukyuans also developed a unique tea ceremony called Buku Buku Cha, a whipped tea made from roasted brown rice.

Music

Ryukyuan music developed from music performed for rites and

ceremonies. The Sanshin (Okinawan samisen) originated from China in the 14th century and influenced songs and dancing. In the 18th century, the Ryukyuan music scoring system called Kururunshi or Kunkunshi was devised. Originally the Sanshin was used by only by the royal court, but its popularity spread throughout the islands and has become the quintessential instrument of Okinawa.

Dance

Ryukyuan Dance evolved out of sacred singing and dancing for religious ceremonies and from the entertaining dances of the common folk. Dancing after the latter era of the Ryukyu Kingdom is divided into the Ryukyuan Classical Dance that developed in the royal court, the "Zo-odori", or Popular Dance, that emerged out of the dissolution of the kingdom in the Meiji Era, and the folk dances handed down regionally since ancient times. Examples of which are the Eisa dances and Shisamai (Chinese lion dances).

Ryukyuan Culture of the Early Modern Age (Arts and Crafts)

Ceramic Art

Ceramics manufacturing in the Ryukyus began when people attempted to reproduce pots imported from the Southeast Asia region during the Ryukyu Kingdom. Korean potters were invited from

Satsuma in the beginning of the 17th century and glazed Joyachi ware started to be produced. It is said that Nakandakari Chigen acquired his techniques in Satsuma and introduced them into Ryukyu in the 18th century. In 1682 three large potteries, Kogachi, Chibana, and Wakuta were consolidated in an area around Makishi in Naha City. The area and pottery produced there became known as Tsuboya.

Lacquerware

Production of lacquerware began in the early days of the 15th century. Under the patronage of successive generations of kings, techniques such as Raden (mother of pearl inlay), Makie (sprinkled pulverized shell), and Chingin (gilt line engraving) were developed. In 1715 the distinctive technique Tsuikin (raised applique decoration) was devised. Lacquerware was used by the upper class aristocrats and as tribute goods for Satsuma. The high humidity of the Okinawan climate is suited for the production of high quality lacquer.

Dyeing and Weaving

Bashofu (banana cloth) is a special product of Okinawa, woven since ancient times. Advanced weaving techniques were being used in Okinawa by the second half of the 16th century. In the latter part of the 16th century on the Sakishima Islands (the Miyako-jima and Yaeyama Island groups) a superior type of ramie (cloth made from

Boehmeria nivea) called Jofu was being produced. Starting in 1610 the inhabitants were obligated to weave this cloth as a tribute item for Satsuma. On Kume-jima Island sericulture was started early on and in the 17th century Tsumugi pongee began to be woven.

Bingata stencil dyed fabric, now the most typical of Okinawa's fabric, was almost completely developed by the 18th century. The techniques of weaving and dyeing in Okinawa were heavily influenced by China and South Asia.

Latter Period Ryukyuan Culture (Residential Housing)

House construction in the kingdom period was controlled by the government. Limits were placed on the residences, living area and building materials according to social rank.

The residences of farmers were called Anaya and limited to 80 tsubo or 264 square meters in area and were with thatched roofs. In Shuri and Naha, genuine wooden houses with tiled roofs called Nuchija were built. After 1889 limits on building were removed and red tiled roofs with the ubiquitous ceramic Shisa (Chinese lion) for protection against natural disaster began appearing. Instead of the typical entrance way or Genkan, found in Japanese houses, a barrier wall called a Hinpun was placed in front and shielded the inside of the main house from view. Looking from the main building, adjacent buildings to the front left were for the newly married and older relatives.

On the right were the animal shed and barn and located in the back was the pigsty. Set around the perimeter of houses were stone walls and Fukugi, garcinias, were planted to prevent typhoon damage

Prehistory of Okinawa

Okinawa lies at the southwest tip of the Japanese archipelago and consists of a chain of a great number of islands. Presently the islands of Okinawa are sandwiched between the Japanese mainland and continental Asia but in ancient times they were connected to the Asian continent. There was migration from the continent by flora and fauna as evidenced by fossils unearthed in excavations.

It is not clear when humans came to inhabit the islands but fossil human bones from the Yamashita-cho Cave 1, excavated in Naha City, have been positively dated to 32,000 years ago and, in Gushigami-son village, the remains of the Minatogawa people have been dated to 17,000 years ago. These Paleolithic humans are thought to have crossed over on a land bridge from continental China but exact details remain unknown.

From the era of the Minatogawa humans there is a blank spot in our knowledge for about 10,000 years until the Neolithic era, around 7,000 years ago. This period in Japan extends through the Jomon Period (to 200BC) and is divided into the Early, First-half, Middle, Late, and Final Jomon Periods and as well as the Yayoi Period (200BC to 250AD). The Early and First-half of the Jomon period was one of thriving exchange between Okinawa and Kyushu. The middle period saw the development of independent cultures on the Okinawa and Amami Islands but the exchanges with Kyushu resumed in the Late Jomon. By the end of the Jomon, villages were forming and there appears to have been contact with China as well. These periods can be said to have been eras of active exchange with Kyushu.

In the Yayoi there are many remains in the coastal sand dunes where artifacts show trade with both Kyushu and China. Shells of Tricornis latissimus shellfish, used as raw material for making shell products, are typical of goods transported to Kyushu at that time. Aside from the earthenware brought in from Kyushu, the custom of burial in box-shaped stone coffins was transferred from Kyushu.

From the Kofun (Tumulus) era (250-552AD) through to the Heian Period (749-1185 AD), the society on the Okinawa and Amami Islands was in the hunter-gatherer stage and there was little contact with mainland Japan.

The Sakishima area, consisting of the Miyako and Yaeyama island groups, formed a different cultural sphere than the Okinawa and Amami island groups. There was no influence from the Jomon and Yayoi cultures and it is thought from existent remains that the Sakishima area had more in common with the southern regions of Asia.

The Paleolithic Age in Okinawa

The Origin of the Ryukyu Island Chain

To the east of continental China, the Ryukyu chain stretches out in the 1,200km between Kyushu and Taiwan. Around the middle of these southern islands is Okinawa Prefecture. The prefecture is composed of 146 islands looking across the vast East China Sea to the continent of China.

From approximately 250 million years ago to 130 million years ago the Ryukyu archipelago was still on the bottom of the ocean. About 15 to 10 million years ago it was connected to Kyushu and continental China. At that time elephants, wild cats and deer migrated across. There have been numerous discoveries such as the so-called living fossil, the Iriomote Island Yamaneko (a wild cat, Mayailurus. Iriomotensis Imaizumi) as well as fossil remains of animals that inhabited the continents of Asia and Japan.

From 10 to 2 million years ago the Ryukyus again separated from other land masses and about 1.5 million years ago, it was connected to continental China. But by 20,000 years ago it had separated completely and broke up into three island groups. By the end of the glacial period the sea level rose 100 meters and the islands became as we see them today

Paleolithic Humans and Culture of the Ryukyu Archipelago

It has been said that humans emerged on earth about 40 million years ago. In Japan, at the Iwajuku site in Gunma Prefecture, flaked stone tools dated about 30,000 years ago have been excavated. In all there are about 5,000 sites in Japan from the Paleolithic age.

While tools have been found in abundance from the Paleolithic era, human remains have not been excavated in any great quantity and there is very little concrete knowledge about the Stone Age humans.

The total picture of Paleolithic humans was made substantially clearer with the discovery of the Minatogawa remains found in 1967 in

Okinawa. It was a complete fossil find showing the skull, hands, and feet of a modern human and was dated to 17.000 years ago. This discovery allowed researchers to get a clear and concrete idea of the appearance of Paleolithic humans and contributed to a great advance in research on the Stone Age.

There have been finds of human fossils in other parts of Okinawa as well; the Yamashita Dojin human in Naha City, the Shimoji-genjin human on Kume-jima Island, and the Pinza-abu human on Miyakojima Island

The Yamashita Dojin and Minatogawa Humans

In 1962 on a Ryukyu limestone plateau on the south side of the Onoyama area of Yamashita-cho, Naha City, in the Yamashita Daiich cave fossilized human remains were discovered. The human fossils excavated here were called the Yamashita Dojin and are believed to be the remains of an 8-year-old girl from 32,000 years ago.

In 1967, in a stone quarry of Gushikami-son, the fossilized remains of 7 Stone Age humans and the fossilized bones of deer and boar were discovered.

The fossils were named after the area where they were found, Minatogawa, and are estimated to be 17.000 years old. The discovery of complete Paleolithic human skeletons with complete skulls, feet and hands were the first such finds in Asia and were of worldwide interest.

The human fossils found at Minatogawa are similar to those of the Peking man (sinanthropus) and the Luijiang human found in continental China. They are said to be the ancestors of the Okinawans living today, but there is much about the Minatogawa humans that remain a mystery. Also there have been very few stone age tools unearthed from Minatogawa sites and details on the lifestyle of these early humans is not known at all.

Fossil Humans and Paleolithic Culture

Within Japan, in the islands of Okinawa, are sites where many human fossils have been discovered.. This is due to the presence of large quantities of calcium carbonate, which leaches out in the substrate water in the Ryukyuan limestone caves of Okinawa. The concentration of calcium carbonate in these stalactite caves has fossilized the bones of humans that were within.

In the digs from other areas of Japan, such as sites in the Kanto region's loam, the acidic nature of the volcanic soil was not conducive to fossilization and most bones dissolved away quickly.

Surveys confirm that there are as many as 600 caves in Okinawa, but most have not been investigated and have been filled in or destroyed. It is desirable to conduct careful study in them because of the possibility of archeological finds within. It is thought that through the advances brought about by investigation and excavation of these stalactite caves, the chances are certain that an increasing number of human fossils will be found.

Name	Estimated Dates	Part of Skeleton Discovered	Year Discovered / Location
Yamashita Dojin	32,0000 years ago	Thighbone of an infant, shinbones, etc.	1962 Naha City
Yonebaru-jin	30,000 years ago (?)	Pelvis, thighbones, clavicle, etc.	1966 Ishigaki City (Ishigaki-shima Island)
Oyama-jin	18,000 years ago	Lower jawbone 1966	Ginowan City
Minatogawa-jin	17,000 years ago	Almost complete skeletons of 4-7 individuals	1967 Gushikami-son
Pinza-abu-jin	26,000 years ago	Parietal and occipital bones	1979 Ueno-son(Miayko-jima Island)
Iegohezu-jin	20,000 years ago	Jawbone, pieces of skull	1977 Ie-son (Iejima Island)
Shimoji-Gendojin	15.000 years ago	Thigh bones of an infant, about 50 pieces of lower jawbone	1983 Gushikawa-son (Kume-jima Island)

The Neolithic Age in Okinawa

The Neolithic Age Cultural Spheres

In the Nanto Islands of the Ryukyu Archipelago there were three prehistoric cultural spheres.

The northern zone comprised Tanegeshima and Yakushima island, of the Satsunan group of islands. The Amami and Ryukyu Island groups comprised the central cultural zone, and the southern zone consisted of the Miyako and Yaeyama island groups.

The Jomon culture of the northern zone moved south into the central zone's Amami and Ryukyu Island groups in the first part of the Jomon period. In those areas there was an independent culture that had already developed and its origin, according to recent archeological excavations, has been found to date from several thousands of years earlier than had previously been thought.

On the other hand, the so-called Sakishima cultural sphere (the Sakishima, Miyako-jima and the Yaeyama Island groups) had a different type of culture than the Jomon and Yayoi cultures of mainland Japan. There were few relations with the Japanese mainland, or the Amami and Okinawa Islands. The Sakishima Islands' roots are deeply related to Taiwan, the Philippines and the southern regions of Asia.

Aspects of Jomon Period Okinawa (1)

Early Jomon(Approx. 10,000 - 8,000 years ago)

Remains from this period consist of the Toguchi Agaribaru ruins of Yomitan-son, the Point B Noguni Shell Mound of Kadena-cho, and the Yabuchi Cave Ruins of Yonashiro-cho. Most of the ruins are situated by the seashore, which indicates a fishing lifestyle for those that lived there. The oldest earthenware pottery in Okinawa is the Tsumegatamon-doki, which have impressions of the makers' fingertips and fingernails on them. This type of pottery is estimated to be around 6,700 years old and is also known as Yabuchi type and Agaribaru type earthenware.

The First-half of the Jomon Period(Approx. 8,000 - 5,000 years ago)
The sites from this period have yielded earthenware produced by Kyushu Jomon peoples and it is thought that boats crossed over from Kyushu bringing these items.

Middle Jomon Period(Approx. 5,000 - 4,000 years ago)
During this period the peoples of the mountainous regions held power in Kyushu and due to this and the enormous amount of volcanic

activity, no Kyushu Jomon culture passed to Okinawa in this period. As a result the prehistoric Nanto central cultural sphere developed its own original culture during this period. Shell mounds have been discovered from this period so it is thought that these people lived in settlements.

Aspects of Jomon Period Okinawa (2)

The Late Jomon Period (Approx. 4000 - 3,000 years ago)

During this period the prehistoric Nanto central cultural sphere developed an independent culture. The biggest influence was the development of the Iha-shiki type and the Ogido-shiki type from the Ichiki-shiki type Kyushu earthenware vessels that had previously been produced. Because of the excavation of dragon and butterfly shaped shell work, it is believed that there were ties with the Chinese continent during this period.

Final Jomon Period (Approx. 3000 - 2,300 years ago)

This period saw the establishment of villages and an increase in the population on the islands. Rudimentary farming was started and excavations have uncovered vessels used for storage. Exchanges with Kyushu occurred frequently and this is believed to have exerted an enormous influence.

Aspects of Yayoi Period Okinawa

Early, Middle, and Late Yayoi Period (Approx. 2,300 - 1,700 years ago)
In this period people who had been living inland on the Ryukyuan limestone hills migrated to the seashore. Excavation of the shell mounds revealed the presence of a large number of giant clam shells used as sinkers leading researchers to believe the people used nets to harvest fish.

The replacement of stone tools for iron and copper utensils from excavations indicate that there was active trading overseas during this period. The Tricornis latissimus and Conidae shells harvested in Amami and Okinawa were transported to Kyushu where they were processed into shell products such as the Kaiwa shell bracelets which were traded throughout the whole of Japan. The products traded for are believed to be Yayoi pottery vessels. The Yayoi period ruins in the prefecture yielded the same type of pottery excavated from Kyushu Yayoi period sites.

The Neolithic Age in Sakishima

Aspects of Neolithic Period Sakishima

In the ruins from prehistoric sites on the islands on the southernmost tip of the Ryukyu archipelago, (the Sakishima. Miyako-jima and Yaeyama Island Groups), there is no apparent influence from Jomon or

Yayoi culture. These islands are believed to have received Philippine and Indonesian influences instead. Perhaps the seas lying between Okinawa and Miyako are the boundary of the Japanese culture's southern expansion.

Contemporary with the Jomon Period (Japan)

Earthenware vessels and stone tools have been found from archeological digs in this period. Pottery of the type designated Shimodabaru, as well as thick reddish brown earthenware without decoration are most typical of vessels from this period. The blades of the stone tools were the only portions of the tools that were polished, unlike those discovered in Okinawa and Amami, so it is thought the primary roots of this culture are from Southeast Asia.

Contemporary with the Yayoi to the Heian Periods (Japan)

Many of the sites from this period can be found near the seashore in sandy areas. The large scale of the culture of this time is its characteristic. Centering on the Yaeyama Islands it extended to the Miyako Islands.

Stone and shell axes have been excavated but the absence of pottery indicates a break with the pottery culture during this period. The use of unsuitable giant clam shells for making axes, examples of which have not been found in Amami and Okinawa, is thought to have been brought over from Southeast Asia and other islands from the south. This period extends from 2,500 BC to the 10th century AD.

The Shell Road

The Nansei Island Group including Okinawa and Amami are formed of beautiful coral reefs. The abundant sea life of the area facilitated the use of shells for making products such as knives, axes, and necklaces. The shells and shell work produced in Okinawa was transported north along the warm Kuroshio current and even reached the mainland of Japan some 2,000 years ago during the Yayoi Period. This has been called "The Shell Road" and is a trading route from the Nansei Island Group northward to the north of Kyushu, past the inland Seto Sea across to the Kinki region of the Japanese mainland. The other route on this Shell Road was up the seacoast of Japan via the Genkainada area off the coast of Kyushu.

Recent excavations in Hokkaido, the northernmost island in Japan, have uncovered shell decoration made in the South Seas, a distance of over 2,000 kilometers. The raw materials, mostly Tricornis latissimus and Conidae shells, were transported to the northern part of Kyushu and shaped into shell products and shipped out all across Japan.

That such a magnificent trading operation was being conducted in the Yayoi is credit to the stable economy of the era and potential for a division of labor that backed it up.

Trading was active along the "The Shell Road" for over 800 years from the Yayoi period (200BC - 250AD) through to the Kofun or Tumulus Period (250 - 552AD). In the Kofun Period the trade brought an increasing variety of shell to the mainland of Japan and the people of Okinawa received grain, products made from metals, and cloth.

Modern Okinawa

The beginning of the 19th century saw the western nations expand nation by nation into Asia. The national seclusion policy was abandoned in Japan and a modern state was established. As part of that process, the Ryukyu Kingdom was incorporated into Japan and the monarchy that had ruled the islands for 500 years was dissolved.

What the future held for the newly established Okinawa Prefecture was down a tumultuous road. Perhaps because of the difference in systems and customs there was a deeply rooted resentment of the old ruling class and the Meiji government in Tokyo. Because of this the Meiji Government adopted the "Ancient Customs Preservation Policy" toward the Ryukyus for the time being.

According to this policy, the landholding system, taxation system, and local government system were all to remain as they were with no great or sudden reforms. This was to avoid any resistance that might come from the Okinawan side. However, the effect of the various policies toward Okinawa resulted in the prefecture falling behind in modernization in comparison to other prefectures and caused the citizens of Okinawa hardships.

The move toward standardizing education to the mainland Japanese standards, along the lines of the Imperial Rescript on Education, began to be thoroughly carried out in the latter half of the 19th century, after the Sino-Japanese War. Subsequent to this, the inexperienced Okinawans were forced into battle in the Russo-Japanese War as members of the Japanese army.

The economic climate in this period of time was that of serious recession. In Okinawa as well, from the latter part of the Taisho Era (1912-1926) to the beginning of the Showa Era (1926-1988) there was widespread economic panic. In this time Okinawans suffered what has been termed the "Cycad Hell", from a type of poisonous palm the people were forced to process and eat to avoid starvation. Many Okinawans opted instead for emigration to mainland Japan and overseas to foreign countries.

As the Showa Era opened, Japanese plans for imperialistic expansion into Asia widened and Okinawa was positioned as the advance base for the defense of the mainland. In March of 1945 it was on the Kerama Island group in Okinawa Prefecture that US Military forces landed and Okinawa entered into the tragic days of the Battle of Okinawa. The Battle of Okinawa resulted in the sacrifice of many people and it can be said to be symbolic of modern Okinawan history shared with mainland Japan.

The Disposition of the Ryukyus

The American Advance in the East

In the start of the 19th century the United States began to consider Japan as a desirable port of call for ships operating in the North Pacific and trading ships going to and from China. In 1846 the US dispatched Commodore Biddle to present demands for opening of Japan but he was turned away by the Tokugawa Shogunate.

The subsequent group dispatched by the US for negotiations with Japan stopped in the Ryukyus before heading to Japan. This time Commodore Perry headed the delegation. The Americans, knowing that the Ryukyu Kingdom was under the control of the Japanese, were thinking of occupying the Ryukyus, should negotiations fail with the Japanese on the mainland. In May 1853 Perry' fleet appeared in the Ryukyus seeking a treaty of commerce with the Ryukyu Kingdom.

While these demands were refused, Perry did succeed in overcoming resistance to a visit to the royal court and he was able to gain admittance to Shurijo Castle.

In June the arrival of Perry's fleet in Uraga on the Japanese mainland resounded throughout Japan. Perry strongly demanded the opening of the country from seclusion and was refused but returned again the following year in March and was able to conclude the Treaty of Kanagawa by a show of strength. In this way the long national seclusion policies of Japan came to an end.

In June of 1854 Commodore Perry again visited the islands and forced the royal court to agree to the "Treaty of Peace and Amity between the Kingdom of the Ryukyus and the United States." The treaty contained provisions prescribing hospitality toward Americans, provisioning of fuel supplies and water, rescue and protection for shipwrecked American sailors, maintenance of the American cemetery, and piloting services.

The Tokugawa Shogunate collapsed under the pressure to open the country from the American and European countries and the modernization of Japan was begun. At the same time this new age became a surging wave in the Ryukyus.

Landfall of American and European Ships on the Ryukyus

1797   British survey ship HMS Providence (Captain William Robert Broughton), Shipwrecked off the coast of the Miyako-Tarama Islands. In the same year the ship headed into Naha Harbor. "A Voyage of Discovery to the North Pacific Ocean" by William Robert Broughton, 1804

1803   British ship HMS Frederick made landfall at Naha Harbor.

1816   British ships Lyra and Alceste arrive in the Ryukyus and stay 42 days. "Account of a Voyage of Discovery to the West Coast of Corea, and the Great Loo-choo Island" London, 1818

1827   British ship HMS Blossom (Captain Frederick Beechey) arrived in the Ryukyus. "Narrative of a Voyage to the Pacific and Beering's Strait" Published 1831

1832   British ship HMS Rodomasuto drifts ashore in the Ryukyus.

1843   British Navy Vessel HMS Samarang makes a land survey of Miyako and Yaeyama Islands. "Narrative Voyage of the HMS Samarang, Published in 1848

1844   French Navy ship Alcmene sails into Naha Harbor seeking friendly relations and trade. Entrusting that a reply to request for trade will be issued to the following ship to call in the Ryukyus, the ship sails on to China leaving behind the missionary Theodore Augustine Focade.

1846   British ship HMS Starling made landfall at Naha Harbor. The English missionary Barnard Bettelheim arrives in the Ryukyus for an 8-year stay. French ship Sabine lands in Naha with Pierre-Julien Le Turdu, successor to Focade. Later the French ships Cleopatoru and Victorious arrive at Unten Harbor seeking reply to the request made in 1844 for friendship and trade relations. They were refused by the Ryukyuans. Visit to Naha of three British fleet vessels. Consent was granted for the start of trade between the Satsuma Han and France.

1847   Ships from western nations visit the Kume-jima, Miyako, Yaeyama and Yonaguni Islands.

1849   British ships arrive requesting commercial relations. . Ships from foreign counties arrive in the Kume-jima and Miyako Islands.

1850   British ship HMS Renard arrives. .

1851   John Manjiro, one of the first Japanese travelers to America arrives. Foreign vessels visit shore in the Ryukyus.

1852   American ship USS Robert Bonn is cast ashore with Chinese laborers.

1853   United States Commodore M.C. Perry arrives in Naha on the Susquehanna and three other ships. Requests are made for free trade with the Ryukyus.

1854   "Treaty of Peace and Amity between the Kingdom of the Ryukyus and the United States." concluded. Russian Admiral Putyatin arrives in the Ryukyus aboard the ship Fregat Pallada. "A Journal of the Perry Expedition to Japan." Published in 1856

The Establishment of the Ryukyu Domain

As Japan opened up and a new government was formed in 1866, the last king of the Ryukyu Kingdom, Sho Tai , had investiture rites performed for his coronation by envoys from China.

In 1871 all of the feudal domains in Japan were abolished and the system of prefectures was established. The Ryukyus were put under the jurisdiction of Kagoshima Prefecture. In 1872 the Meiji government on the mainland summoned envoys and announced that Sho Tai had been appointed King of the Ryukyu Domain.

This was the start of what is called the "Disposition of the Ryukyus".

The Ryukyuan government only understood that this event meant that jurisdiction over the Ryukyus was being transferred from Satsuma to the central government in Tokyo. They did not take notice that the important point of this was the dissolution of the Ryukyu Kingdom.

The Meiji government, wanting to avoid confrontation with the Ryukyuans and Chinese did not immediately implement the dissolution of the domains as it had with the rest of Japan. Instead they took a step by step approach toward the dissolution of the kingdom by naming Sho Tai the "king", not "lord", of a domain.

Dissolution of the Domains and Establishment of the Prefectures

In 1875 the Meiji government formulated policy contained in the edict entitled the "Disposition of the Ryukyus". It conveyed the government's policy of dismantling the Ryukyu Domain and annexing it as Okinawa Prefecture. In the same year it dispatched an official to take charge of the dissolution, Michiyuki Matsuda. His orders were to:

1. Abolish the tributary relationship with China and break off Ryukyuan relations with China.

2. Dispatch young public officials to study the new governmental and educational systems.

3. Reform the administration and institutions under the model of the other prefectures.

4.Establish a military garrison so that the reforms could be conducted without disturbances.

Having received notice of these measures, the Ryukyuan Court, without instituting any countermeasures of their own, simply appealed to the Japanese government to be allowed to continue to conduct the dual tributary relationship with China and Japan it had up until then. Rule in the court was multi-layered and many were simply afraid that by being annexed as part of Japan they would lose land, status and assets.

The Meiji government, deciding that it was unable to understand what the response of the court would be through persuasion, issued an edict authorizing the apprehension of the King.

In March of 1879, after receiving his orders to "abolish the Ryukyu Kingdom and establish Okinawa Prefecture", Matsuda, with police and army units in tow, landed in the Ryukyus and communicated what he was to do to the Ryukyuan court. Through this action all of the land, citizens, and all related documents of the court administration of the former Ryukyuan Royal Court were to be turned over to the Meiji government. Sho Tai, the former king, was given a degree of nobility and ordered to reside in Tokyo. The 500-year rule of the Ryukyu Kingdom was destroyed by these actions.

The Ryukyus and Okinawa

The Chinese used the term Ryukyus in many documents over the course of history. The currently used Chinese characters for the Ryukyus came into use when King Satto of the central Chuzan Kingdom established relations with Ming China in the 14th century.

The current Chinese characters used to designate the prefecture Okinawa came from the name the local people called their own island (Uchina in Okinawan dialect). It was first used in documentation in Japan in the "Tale of the Heike" by Nagato.

There are some historians and who believe the first historical use was a place called "Aji-Naha-to" in the "Todaiwa Joto Seiden." There are also references to Okinawa as "Akina" as well.

The name Okinawa can be found in documents from the Shimazu domain in the 17th century and in Arai Hakuseki's "Nantoshi". In this book Okinawa is written with the current characters and it is therefore said to have been in common use.

When the edict dismantling the Ryukyu Kingdom was issued and the domains were abolished, the prefectural system was established and the Ryukyu Domain was named Okinawa Prefecture because the name Ryukyu came from the Chinese.

The Miyako and Yaeyama Separation from Okinawa

Issues concerning the Ryukyus were not completely solved by dissolving the domains and institution of the prefecture system. China did not recognize this action and there were repeated requests from the Ryukyus for assistance from China.

United States President U. S. Grant was asked by Chinese authorities to help solve the dispute. He held meetings with high Japanese officials such as Ito Hirobumi to try and negotiate. The proposal put forth by the Japanese delegation was that in exchange for recognition of trade and commercial rights within China, similar to those enjoyed by the European countries, the Chinese would take control of the Yaeyama and Miyako Islands. This was the so so-called "Divided Islands / Expanded Treaty" proposal. .

Negotiations ran into difficulties but, with China preoccupied in border disputes with Russia, it agreed to the terms of the treaty anyway.

In February 1881, representatives from both nations were to meet on Ishigaki-jima Island and sign the treaty officially separating the Yaeyama and Miyako Islands and ceding them to China.

However, before formal ratification China experienced internal revolts and fearing the danger of Japanese incursions into Asia refused to conclude the treaty. Also, perhaps because of the influence of repeated requests from Ryukyuans exiled to China, the treaty was shelved.

In 1872 the Ryukyu Domain was established and in 1879 the domain was replaced with the establishment of Okinawa Prefecture. Through this the political process passed from the "Divided Islands / Expanded Treaty" toward what is called the "Disposition of the Ryukyus."

After this, the Japanese advances into Korea led to confrontation with China, which then led to the Sino-Japanese War (1894-1895). With the Japanese victory in this war, Taiwan became a colony of Japan and the "Ryukyu Problem" faded as they were annexed as part of Japan.

Okinawa's Civil Rights Movement

Ancient Customs Preservation Policy

In 1879 when Okinawa Prefecture was established, Naoyoshi Nabeshima, dispatched from the central government, was made governor of the prefecture. After that all the important posts in the Okinawa Prefecture government were entrusted not to Okinawans, but to mainland Japanese. This was the shift to the Yamatoyu, or Japanese world.

The major policy of the Meiji government toward Okinawa was that while changes such as the abolition of the court bureaucracy and monarchial social positions were carried out, many of the systems were allowed to remain. This was the "Ancient Customs Preservation Policy" and it meant that older systems such as the land allocation, taxation, and local governmental would remain as they had been. This was an attempt to avoid sudden drastic reforms and it was a direction policy took for some time .

There are a number of reasons for this policy including not wanting to invite revolt by the old ruling class in the Ryukyus, the turmoil of the domestic government in the midst of change, and the enormous profit gained by just taking over the existing tax system.

However, the policy was one of the great causes for delays in the modernization of Okinawa.

While the Meiji government offered some guaranteed stipends to the samurai, they were extended only to those registered as descendants of samurai, a small portion of the warrior class. Stipends were not extended to the large majority of low-level unregistered samurai who received very little in the way of economic support during these changes. Many of them were forced to begin new occupations as merchants and farmers. Numerous accounts described the pitiful conditions of the ruined samurai.

The Farmers Movements

When the Meiji government first began implementing the dissolution of the domains, it announced it would reduce the heavy taxation carried out under the old regime. But in reality what the people received under the new system of taxation was the "Preservation of Ancient Customs" policy that was essentially unchanged from the days of the monarchy.

The collapse of the old feudal authority in Shuri however, did most certainly affect the awareness of the people. The common folk, the farmers, began by themselves to insist on guarantees for subsistence.

Anger exploded in many regions at the ruling classes as they used the patently unfair policy to shield themselves. .

On Aguni-jima Island in 1881, farmers, in solidarity, denounced the unjust tax collection of the village officials. In 1883, in Yabu-son village of the Nago district, the farmers demanded the release of the property of the affluent Kugoke houses. Resistance broke out against the unfair policies of the village officials throughout Okinawa. To control the democratic movement brewing in Okinawa, the governor, Michitoshi Iwamura issued a prohibition against protests but the anger of the farmers could not be suppressed.

This type of farmer's protest was directed primarily at the unjust regional officials and taxes and expressed resistance and dissatisfaction with the policy of "Preservation of the Ancient Customs". The movement did not take the form of anything but declarations demanding reform.

The protest movement did have enough influence on the prefectural authorities to get a farmer's representative the right to participate in the budget deliberations in 1888. With the movement to abolish the per capita tax on Miyako-jima Island the protests reached a peak.

The Movement to Abolish the Per Capita Tax

The retention of the per capita tax under the "Preservation of Ancient Customs" policy reduced the residents of Miyako to even deeper poverty. The protest movement that had spread throughout the whole of Okinawa Prefecture sparked a campaign to abolish the head tax in Miyako.

Sugar farming engineer, Seian Gusukuma, and trader Jisaku Nakamura were witness to the suffering and agony of the farmers and were essential in establishing the protest movement in Miyako.

The two headed the list of signatories on the Miyako farmers petition to reduce the number of officials in the regional bureaucracy and abolish the per capita tax. The petition was addressed to the newly appointed Governor Shigeru Narahara . Due to strong resistance from the samurai class the petition was put aside and the result was further an increase in the confrontation between the farmers and the privileged samurai.

The farmers, under the guidance of Gusukuma and Nakamura, submitted the petition again, and because it appeared it would not be accepted, made plans to travel to Tokyo and make a direct appeal to the Imperial Diet. On the way to the capital the samurai and police harassed them but they succeeded in handing the appeal regarding the current status of farmers within Miyako to the Secretary for Home Affairs.

In this way the perseverance of the farmers finally paid off in 1903 when the per capita tax was revoked.

However it should not be overlooked that at the time when they submitted the petition to the 8th Imperial Diet in 1895, Japan was in the midst of the Sino-Japanese War and the central government's belief in the urgent need to modernize Okinawa and integrate the defense of the nation was a reason the government abolished the per capita tax. However, despite this, the fact that the Miyako Farmers Movement did spur the Meiji government and lead the way to a reform of the "Preservation of Ancient Customs" policy makes this worthy of mention due to its effect on the modern history of Okinawa Prefecture.

Noboru Jahana and the Prefectural Government Reform Movement

As the demands to reform the old customs of privilege grew along with the democratic movement in Okinawa, the prefectural authorities were obliged to make moves on the reforms.

When the prefecture's governor during that period, Shigeru Narahara, took office he permitted the reclamation of the Somayama lumber forests managed in common by the farmers under the old royal government and provided relief measures for the poverty stricken lower class samurai families. The push for these reforms came from Noboru Jahana, born in a farming family and one of the first prefectural scholarship students to be sent to the mainland for study.

There were voices heard that this reform would lead to the destruction of the forests and a shortage of resources because of over-harvesting. However, Jahana persuaded the farmers that the cultivation of the land was necessary to bring relief to the poor samurais and if it was made arable and was in a place where it would bring no significant damage to the forests

But the reality of this reform was that it was for the lower-class samurai in name only and the powerful samurai families, Japanese merchants from the mainland, and the top-level officials were given priority in the disposal of the land. The discrimination of the Narahara government toward the Okinawans (Uchinanchu) led Jahana to distrust the leadership and resign his position in the government. He founded a political organization, the Okinawa Club, to oppose the Narahara government. At the same time Jahana developed campaigns for autonomy, suffrage for Okinawans, and reforms of the autocratic style of government.

He persistently attacked the Narahara administration which, together with the old ruling elite, responded by using their political power to oppress the activities of the Okinawa Club. The constant pressure led to the breakup of the organization. Noburu Jahana, penniless and without work, died in misfortune in 1898.

There is much about the work of Jahana and the civil rights movement that is unclear and any evaluations of them remain unsettled. It can be said however that he organized the first political group in Okinawa that centered on the peasants and farmers and had great significance through his attempts to have this reflected in the policies of the prefectural administration.

Reformation of Old Customs and Abolition of Special Institutions

Land Adjustment Practices

The most notable of the reasons for the poverty that Okinawa experienced after the modernization was the retention of the old land allocation system. The land system of Okinawa was a regional allocation system which did not, in principle, allow private ownership of land. The farmers paid tax imposed on the land with tax exceptions given to the richer samurai class and the system was full of inconsistencies.

The movements to abolish the per capita tax and against the unfair tax collection practices by local tax officials came about through the power of the peasant farmers themselves. These movements overlapped with the work of people like Noboru Jahana in the suffrage movement by trying to force reform in land allocation and taxation on the Meiji government.

The Meiji government saw the need for a stable tax system and rational government rule as essential to the transition to a modern capitalist nation and so for these reasons as well the reform of the old systems was an indispensable.

Land adjustments, comparable to the ones carried out in mainland Japan between 1873-1879, were started in Okinawa in 1899 and completed by 1903. The main points of the reform were a recognition of the ownership of the land by the individual farmer originally using that land, that landowners were to be the taxpayers, the abolishment of the per capita tax, and that land tax was to be fixed at 2.5% of the land value. To a certain extent the tax burden was eased but due to increases in the national tax and establishment of new taxes the actual tax burden became heavier as time went on.

However, the land adjustments did have a large impact on the lives of the peasant farmers. Prior to reforms the land was allocated arbitrarily, the crops cultivated were strictly controlled, and tax was made by payment in kind. After the reforms the farmers owned their land and were free to plant what they wanted and tax was regulated. The cultivation of the sole cash crop, sugarcane, spread.

Many farmers suffered under the heavy tax payments and some had to leave their lands and work. Different classes of farmers developed, those without land had no choice either to become employed as tenant farmers or emigrate outside the prefecture or even outside of Japan to find work.

Regional Political Reform and National Government Participation

One more pivotal aspect of the old system preceding the land adjustments was the reorganization of regional governments carried out in 1896. According to this reorganization Okinawa was divided into five counties or districts. These were the Shimajiri, Nakagami, Kunigami, Miyako, and Yaeyama districts and the central urban areas of Naha and Shuri were divided into two wards.. The first three of the districts were assigned district heads and the Sakishima Islands (the Sakishima, Miyako, and Yaeyama Island groups) were assigned island heads. Naha and Shuri were placed under the control of district heads. This clarified the administrative boundaries.

In 1897 the Magiri and Shimabandokoro offices were renamed as government offices and the number of personnel was greatly reduced. . Furthermore, in 1899, a meeting of the island and district assemblies was called whose members were selected by representatives of the islands and districts.

While this was a step toward autonomy, this assembly was not entirely independent of the prefectural authorities. Reforms leading to a more complete regional autonomy would take another 10 years.

In 1908 the jurisdictional suffixes denoted by the words Magiri and Shima were changed to Cho (Town) and Son (Village). Areas previously denoted by Son were changed to Aza. In the following year, 1909, the prefectural assembly was established but there were still many limitations on its authority. It was not until 1920 at the height of the Taisho democracy that the people of Okinawa enjoyed a similar degree of autonomy as the other prefectures of Japan. The activities of Noboru Jahana calling for participation by Okinawa in the National Diet took until 1912 to be implemented. The participation of Miyako and Yaeyama was not allowed until 1919.

The Implementation of a Conscript Military

The Meiji government, aiming at a "Prosperous Nation, Strong Army", modernized the military along the lines of Western military structure and an obligatory military service was instituted with the promulgation of the Military Conscription Ordinance in 1873.

Planning for the application of this edict in Okinawa began in 1885. By 1896 military service was implemented for primary school teachers and two years later it was applied to the general population. The motivation for conscription of schoolteachers first was to implement an ideological system for indoctrinating loyalty to the emperor in his subjects so that the teachers would then pass on the ideals of military education to the students they taught.

The public servants, educators, and newspaper journalists of Okinawa greeted institution of military conscription as a way the prefecture's citizens could at last be admitted into the circle of citizens of Imperial Japan. The ordinary citizens of Okinawa however saw this in a different light and sought a myriad of ways to avoid military service, from becoming fugitives to feigning disabilities. The number of persons jailed for draft evasion in the first 18 years of conscription was 744 persons.

And those that chose to enter found because many of them spoke no or very little Japanese that there was considerable discrimination against them by mainland Japanese. Having been instilled with the Imperial ideology and as Japanese citizens, there was very little that Okinawans could do to transcend the discrimination they found, except to prove themselves in the battlefield with their blood. The soldiers of Okinawa, unable to change the perceptions of them, finally entered combat in the Russo-Japanese war. The casualty rate for them was around ten percent. Their sacrifice earned them the praise of the Japanese government as true subjects of the Japanese emperor.

Those Okinawans who had turned their backs to the Meiji government over the Sino-Japanese War joined in on the Russo-Japanese War in the spirit of "Chukun- Aikoku" (Loyalty to the Emperor and Patriotism) and started down the way to becoming citizens of the modern Japan.

Education and Academics in Modern Okinawa

The first governor dispatched to Okinawa, Naoyoshi Nabeshima, instituted policies to quickly bring the culture and language into line with standards in Japan. For this reason, Okinawa Teachers' School was established in 1880, the year following the establishment of the prefecture. It was the first such school in Okinawa. As reorganization progressed modern education was introduced through the Okinawa Prefectural elementary and junior high schools.

Initially school attendance was low due to resistance to Japanese rule. In 1887 attendance by girls was permitted. During the Sino-Japanese War attendance remained low at 30% but from the Russo-Japanese War until 1927 attendance steadily rose toward the 99% mark.

By 1900, junior high school education was effected for girls. Public and private schools for girls, vocational schools, and medical training schools were established. However higher education systems, senior high schools and universities were not established and so the leadership level of Okinawan natives did not progress.

The number of young people aiming for careers in academics by traveling to the mainland for higher education gradually increased. Of particular note is the scholar Fuyu Iha who put the highest priority on research concerning the original qualities of Okinawan culture in an age when the rush was to throw aside those practices to conform to Japanese standards.

He protested the discriminatory education against Okinawa in junior high school and continually searched for "a way to live and be Okinawan." After quitting school he went to Tokyo University and studied linguistics, conducting research on the Omoro-soushi, the ancient compilation of ballads and song from the Okinawa and Amami Islands. Not active only in the field of linguistics, he also studied history as well as ethnic studies and conducted comprehensive research on Okinawa throughout his life. Starting with his first book "Koryukyu" (The Ancient Ryukyus) published in 1911, he penned numerous writings on Okinawa related subjects and has since been called the "Father of Okinawan Studies".

Other great scholars from Okinawa included Kanjun Higashionna who wrote "Nanto Fudoki" (Topography of the Southern Islands) as well as

Toso Miyara who conducted thorough linguistic studies of all the dialects in Japan. There were others as well that have left behind an impressive body of research that has stimulated studies on Okinawa.

The Society and Culture of Modern Okinawa

As reforms continued, they brought with them a new and modern Okinawan culture.

In 1893 the first newspaper, The Ryukyu Shimpo, was started and soon many others began publishing as well. While these newspapers all competed for their own development and special interests, they fulfilled a vital role in the debates about government policy and brought new enlightening ways of thinking to the public.

In literature, 1904 saw a Ryukyuan culture and arts renaissance which included the expression of modern viewpoints by such men as Getsujo Iha and many others who wrote for various Japanese literary magazines. Seichu Yamashiro, who had exchanges with the famous poets Akiko and Tekkan Yosano, produced numerous works published within the mainland literary world. Others active in the Taisho period (1912-1926) include Kunio Serei and Sekiho Ikemiyagi and in the Showa period (1926-1988) there was Eikichi Yamazato and Nantestsu Iba. One of the better known of these was Baku Yamanoguchi, who went to Tokyo and lived as a starving artist to write witty poems full of humor and pathos.

In painting, the traditional arts patronized by the old court were preserved and developed but also there was a great influx of Japanese and Western art techniques . Shozan Nakazone, known as an official royal court painter and artist Kakoku Nagamine continued to paint in the traditional styles after the Meiji period began. They also incorporated the new techniques to create their own originality. Seiraku Nishime traveled to Tokyo Art School to learn the techniques of Western painting so that he and his fellow teacher Keijo Higa could pass these new techniques on to the younger generation of painters in Okinawa.

In music the traditional Okinawan music was categorized as Ryukyuan classical music and is the subject of study to this day. Choho Miyara introduced elements of Western music into these compositions and formed a new fusion with the classical Okinawan genre to create popular songs such as "Endo-no Hana" and "Nanta-hama". He was also a teacher of music at a teacher's school.

Performing arts for the public at large were began by those artists who had been schooled as performers for the royal court but had lost their employment when the court was dissolved. They were known as

Shibaishi and through such plays as "Shurijo Hirakewatashi" and operas such as "Tumaiaka" gained reputations as public performers. The older forms of Ryukyuan theater arts such as Ryukyuan Classical Dance and Kumiodori (classical theater) were passed on to the younger performers but it is said there were few opportunities to play them before the public.

Life in Okinawa During the "Cycad Hell"

The Life of Okinawan Citizens During the "Cycad Hell"
After the Russo-Japanese War, Japan experienced a deep economic recession and it was not until the outbreak of WWI in 1914 that things improved because the European powers withdrew from the region leaving Japan in a monopoly position in the Asian market. Economic activity recovered by the export of munitions, iron products and medicines and there was an industrial resurgence in Japan. Okinawa also received the benefits of the upswing by exporting products such as sugar, the profits of which were so great the newly rich were called "Sugar Rich" at the time.

The economic boom during the First World War did not last forever. After WWI the European powers again advanced on the Asian market and Japan's exports plummeted. A domestic surplus of output caused a post-war depression. In Okinawa the price of sugar fell and a wave of depression washed over the islands.

In 1923 the Great Kanto Earthquake and the worldwide effects of the Great Depression caused a chronic economic downturn known as the "Showa Depression" in Japan and this seriously affected the lives of Okinawans as well.

The economic depression that gripped Okinawa from the final years of the Taisho era was named "Sotetsu-jigoku", or "Cycad hell", after a poisonous plant in the palm family the people were forced to process and eat to avoid starvation. Over 70% of the population during this period were farmers and due to the depression, their staples, rice and potatoes, became scarce and they were forced to eat the indigenous plants to survive. Despite the poisonous nature of the plant and the possibility of it causing death if the poison was not completely removed by repeated processing, the impoverished farmers used it to overcome starvation.

Taxes were still collected despite the poverty of the farmers and this combined with the yearly typhoons and occasional droughts made life hell for the Okinawans. Many were forced to sell relatives and others migrated overseas or to mainland Japan in search of work.

Emigration and Employment Overseas

As Okinawa is an island prefecture with scarce arable land , the poor of Okinawa sought a means of escape by overseas emigration.

In 1899 the first 26 immigrants from Okinawa were dispatched to Hawaii under the efforts of Kyuzo Toyama and in the seven years after, over 4670 joined them in their immigration, most of them to Hawaii. The Okinawans seeking to escape the Cycad Hell occupied over 10% of the Japanese who immigrated in the years between 1923 and 1930.

The funds sent from overseas back to Okinawa gave significant and much needed support for their families and aided the economy of Okinawa as a whole. While there were some great success stories, most of those who went to work overseas had to endure hardships while continuing to work.

In addition to those working overseas, there were many Okinawans who moved to the mainland to find work. Most of the immigrants to the mainland settled in the Kobe-Osaka region and worked in the spinning and weaving industries. Many worked in appalling conditions and were humiliated by the discrimination against Okinawans.

Many formed organizations and associations of Okinawans as peer support seeking to raise the appalling living standards of Okinawan workers. They survived and got stronger.

Okinawa Social Movement

In the capitalist but underdeveloped Okinawa, the socialist theories of class struggle and labor movement spread from people that had gone to the mainland of Japan to work.

In the early 1900's the ideas of socialism spread to the educators and intelligentsia and on other levels of society. Disputes between tenant farmers and landowners erupted frequently.

In 1926 leaders of the mainland Socialist movement formed the Okinawa Seinen Domei (Okinawa Youth Alliance) and coordinated a strike of the labor unions in various professions. In the first general election in Japan in 1928 (only males 25 and older were franchised), the socialist leaders ran in the election and the activities of the party picked up.

The student movements and teacher unions were also very active. Okinawan citizens attending university in Tokyo and senior high teachers' school intensified their activities and more than a few were dismissed or punished. Around 1930 the teacher's unions were formed on Yaeyama and the main island of Okinawa.

The response of the authorities to the intensified activities of the socialists was to exert control by using special police units that began an unfair crackdown on various socialist movement activities. In the middle 1930's many student and movement leaders were jailed and were forcibly deported from Okinawa. By 1940 the social movements in Okinawa were facing one of their most difficult periods.

The Dialect Controversy and Imperialist Education

Together with the end of the Sino-Japanese War and the wave of modernization, there were moves to bring the culture and manners of the Okinawans into line with that of mainland Japan. In the first decade of the Showa era (1926-1988) this activity increased, even to the extent of having people change the pronunciation of the characters in their names to sound more Japanese.

The pending issue of rigid enforcement of the use of standard Japanese intensified as nationalist sentiment grew. In 1940 the prefectural authorities promoted enforcement of the use of standardized Japanese thorough such measures as coercion and prohibition as they took steps to "Eradicate Okinawan Dialect". The presence of such people as the Japan Folk Craft Association's Muneyoshi Yanagi (Soetsu Yanagi) in Okinawa who criticized the enforcement as going too far, ignited debates about dialect both in and outside the prefecture.

This controversy did not result in any definite conclusion but the enforcement of a unified system in Japan only got more coercive as Japan began the road to militarism and war. When the battle for Okinawa began the Japanese army regarded anyone using Okinawan dialect as a spy and used severe pressure on those who used it. During the battle there incidents where the use of dialect resulted in tragedy for those who used it.

The viewpoints of Yanagi and others began to have more influence after the war when reflection on the problems caused by contempt for Okinawans and the idea that Okinawa could simply be made to follow Japan. Reflection on these lead to reaffirmation of the richness of Okinawan culture.

The Battle of Okinawa

Evacuations and the 10/10 Air Raid

From the first days of the Asia- Pacific war, Okinawa was fortified as the location of airbases and as the frontline in the defense of mainland Japan. Land and farms were forcibly expropriated throughout Okinawa and the Imperial Japanese Army began the construction of airbases.

In 1944, the 32nd Army of Okinawa was established and fighting units of the military were dispatched to the Okinawa Islands and the

Sakishima Islands (Sakishima Island and the Miyako and Yaeyama Island groups). In the areas to which they were dispatched, the local schools and houses were used as garrisons and the local farmers were required to provide logistical supplies from their own food and domesticated animals.

As the war entered its final stage, the fall of Saipan Island, home to so many immigrants from Okinawa, had a deep impact on the people of Okinawa. Not only sorrow because of the loss of fellow countrymen but also dread knowing that the next target of the advance would be Okinawa.

In order to fight a protracted war using Okinawa as a frontline, the young, old, and infirm were evacuated from the prefecture. The Japanese government made plans to evacuate 80,000 Okinawans to mainland Japan and 20,000 to Taiwan but because of reluctance to go to an unknown land and the presence of enemy ships in the seas near Okinawa, the plans were not fully implemented. Incidents such as the torpedoing of the Tsushima Maru, which was carrying 1700 passengers, including 800 school children , heightened the anxiety surrounding evacuation considerably.

However, after the 10/10 Air Raid attacks on October 10, 1944, the number of those willing to chance evacuation increased greatly.

The 10/10 Air Attack, so called because it took place in the tenth month on the tenth day was a massive aerial bombardment of the entire Nansei Island region by the U. S. Military. Attacks were made on the Amami-jima islands in the north to Ishigaki-jima Island in the south and Daito-jima Island in the east. In Naha City the fierce attack burned out 90% of the buildings in the city and many priceless cultural treasures of the Ryukyuan Kingdom were lost. The air attack consisted of 1400 aircraft and inflicted 600 deaths and 700 injuries.

The Start of the Battle of Okinawa

In Okinawa, starting in 1943, military drills taught in the junior high school were intensified. . In July of the same year Prime Minister Hideki Tojo visited Okinawa, in November nurse training for girl students was begun and the student mobilization system was fully established.

After the air raids of October 10, 1945, mobilization of the students intensified, evacuation of students was no longer permitted and a system was prepared so the schools could give complete support to the armed forces. In February of 1945, male teachers and students from the middle and teaching schools were organized into the Imperial Blood and Iron Corps and the women and girls were organized into the Himeyuri Nurse Corps as nurses attached to the Japanese Haebaru infantry field hospital on the battlefields.

After the first massive bombing on September 10, 1944, the beginning of the New Year saw further intensification of the air attacks by the US forces and the conquest of Okinawa was only a matter of time.

On March 26, 1945 the U.S. forces landed on the Kerama Islands. The dreadful ground war was begun.

Most of the units stationed in the Kerama Islands were marine volunteers and special attack units, there were hardly any infantry troops there at all . Due to the sudden landing by U.S. forces on Kerama, the Japanese troops fled to hide in caves in the middle mountainous part of the island. After resisting as hard as they were able, the volunteer forces were completely crushed. The civilians were given orders directly and indirectly to commit suicide to avoid capture. Many civilians, with no place to escape to and in ignorant fear of the American troops, gathered together and killed themselves and their relatives and children in group suicides. In the Kerama islands the death toll from these group suicides was 329 people for Tokashiki-jima Island, 171 persons on Zamami-jima Island, and on Geruma-jima Island it was 53 people.

Progress of the Battle of Okinawa

On April 1, 1945, U.S. military forces landed at Yomitan, Kadena and Chatan in the middle part of the main island of Okinawa without experiencing any resistance or casualties. They immediately occupied two former airfields of the Japanese forces. The main reason for the lack of resistance was that the transfer of troops to other locations had left them short in Okinawa and the Japanese had to shift their strategy from a shoreline defense to plans for a protracted holding action. The strategy was that if the U.S. forces could be delayed in their conquest of Okinawa, the mainland of Japan would have more time to become sufficiently prepared for a decisive battle there.

On April 2, the day after landing, the U.S. forces reached the eastern seacoast and divided the island in two. By April 20th they had substantially effected occupation of the entire northern area. The civilians hiding in the mountainous areas, weakened by malaria and starvation, had not only the bullets of the U. S. forces to fear, but also needed to protect themselves from the plundering, torture and massacres committed by the remaining Japanese soldiers.

The battles up in the northern part of the island around the airfield on Ie-jima Island were particularly fierce. In the six days of intense fighting many civilians as well as soldiers lost their lives. Over 100 of the civilians died in group suicides.

In the mid-southern areas the defending Japanese forces attacked the U.S. forces in heated battles for a few days but after losing over half of their fighting units suffered complete defeat. On May 27, 1945 the units of the Japanese army defending Okinawa retreated from their underground headquarters in Shuri to Mabuni in the southern part of the island. Finding the caves already occupied by civilian refugees, the Japanese forces ejected them, requisitioned the refugee's supplies and in some cases executed them.

As the Japanese forces retreated in battle from their airfield in Oroku, Rear Admiral Minoru Ota, after noting the bravery of the Okinawans supporting the Imperial Navy units there sent a telegram saying , "Thus fought the Okinawans, and I ask you to consider these prefectural citizens as meriting future reward." After this he committed suicide and the army was crushed.

The Japanese forces retreated to the southernmost tip and after losing the final battle on June 22 (some accounts say June 23), the commander, Lt. General Mitsuru Ushijima and Chief of Staff, Isamu Cho, committed suicide and all organized resistance was finished. Pockets of resistance continued to fight the U.S. forces, even after the

Battle of Okinawa was finished on July 2, 1945. It was not until September 2, 1945 that the head of the remaining Japanese forces on the island signed formal surrender.

War on the Sakishima and Other Island Groups

During the Battle of Okinawa, the other islands where the U.S. forces did not land such as on the Sakishima Islands (Sakishima, Miyako-jima Island, and the Yaeyama Island group) also experienced great sacrifices.

On Sakishima there was considerable damage from the aerial bombardment of the U.S. and British navies but, the most serious damage was caused by lack of food and malaria.

On Yaeyama, the people were forced to leave their homes and go into the mountainous areas. 3,647 people, about 11% of the population, contracted and died of malaria. The six thousand residents of Miyako-jima Island had over three thousand troops stationed there and suffered extreme food shortages and malaria.

On Izena-jima Island on the northern coast of the Okinawa mainland, three U.S. servicemen cast ashore were executed under orders by Japanese soldiers, who then went on to kill the nearby villagers. The islands of Iheya-jima and Aguni-jima had no Japanese troops stationed there and the U.S. forces landed smoothly and there were effectively no great losses of life. Residents were able to surrender smoothly to U. S. forces as a result. The presence or absence of Japanese troops determined the extent of the casualties suffered by the civilian residents. On the small island Sesoko-jima, on the north coast of Okinawa, the residents, fearing the casualties caused by the presence of Japanese troops, repelled the Japanese soldiers that had crossed over to escape from the main island.

The presence of bomber base on Tsuken-jima in the Nakagusuku Gulf meant that this area became one of intense fighting. On Tonaki-jima Island, communications were cut with the mainland of Okinawa, residents were forced to endure starvation until the news of the end of the war reached there in the middle of September.

Post-War Okinawa

On August 15,1945 Japan signed the Potsdam Declaration, ending World War Two after fighting for fifteen years. The Allied forces occupied Japan and the Nansei Islands were put under U.S. military rule.

The United Nations was founded centering on the nations that had won in WWII, but a new kind of international tension arrived with the

Cold War competition between the West, allies of the United States, and the East, centered on the Soviet Union. With the intensification of the Cold War and the establishment of socialist governments in China and North Korea, the U.S. came to regard the geographic position of Okinawa as strategically important and the basis for a long term rule over the islands became a fixed policy.

In 1949, with long-term rule in mind, the military government implemented economic reconstruction and democratic government, consolidated the military facilities, began planning for permanent bases and granted a certain degree of self-autonomy to the residents of Okinawa. In December of the following year, the strong direct government of the U.S. Navy was replaced by the United States Civil Administration of the Ryukyu Islands (USCAR) but overall control remained unchanged and was retained by the military.

In 1951 the San Francisco Peace Treaty and the U.S. Japan Security Treaty were concluded and Japan regained independence, but the islands of Okinawa remained under the authority of the U.S. Government. As Japan joined the other nations of the West, Okinawa became a stronghold in the fight against the communists of China, North Korea, and the Soviet Union.

With the international situation such as it was, the bases on Okinawa underwent full-scale strengthening. In 1953 The U.S. Civil Administration began land expropriations in support of the strengthening of the bases. The Okinawan resistance to the land requisitions was strong, igniting an "island-wide struggle" whose momentum continued to gather steam under the "Reversion Movement."

In 1965 Japanese Prime Minister Eisaku Sato visited Okinawa and began to press for the return of Okinawa to Japan. Okinawa's reversion to Japan was realized on May15, 1972. Still 25 years since the reversion to Japan, Okinawa, occupying only 1% of the land area of Japan, is the location of 75% of the U.S. military bases in Japan. There remain many issues concerning the bases.

Defeat and U.S. Occupation

The Start of U.S. Occupation

In March 1945 the U.S. forces that landed on the Kerama Islands issued the Nimitz Declaration suspending all the political rights of the Japanese Imperial Government and declared the Nansei Islands under the jurisdiction of the Untied States Navy. From that date, Okinawa was severed from Japan for 27 years until the reversion on May 15,

1972. Okinawa experienced a very different kind of postwar life than did the mainland of Japan.

On April 1, 1945 the U.S. forces landed in the Hija area of Yomitan-son and began to establish military rule throughout the Nansei Islands.

In August of the same year Japan signed the Potsdam Declaration, ending the war. On that same day, at the invitation of the U.S. military government, Okinawan leaders from the internment camps held meetings in Ishikawa City in the central area of mainland Okinawa. This was the first democratic assembly of residents in postwar Japan. The result of that meeting was the formation of the "Okinawa Advisory Council." Mr. Koshin Shikiya was chosen to head the assembly. On April of the following year the Council became the Okinawa Civil Government, thus the Okinawan Legislature was established.

However, the military government appointed all the governor and assembly members. After that rule shifted from the U.S. Navy to the U.S. Army, and later on to the U.S. Civil Administration, but real power rested with the U.S. military.

Various Postwar

The Okinawan War Memorial Day is on June 23, the day of the suicide of Lt. Gen. Mitsuru Ushijima, commander of the 32nd Imperial Japanese Army. (Ushijima's suicide actually took place the day before on June 22nd.). But it was not the day the Battle of Okinawa ended. Confrontations between the United States military and Imperial Japanese forces continued after June 23rd.

The U.S. forces announced the end of the battle on July 2, 1945, but pockets of resistance from isolated Imperial Japanese troops continued. The strategies for getting them under control continued even after the surrender of Japan on August 15, 1945. As a result, substantial conflicts occurred until the formal surrender of the remaining Japanese forces on September 7, 1945.

In June of the same year, even as the battles were still being conducted on Okinawa, the first schools opened in the internment camps of each region and classes were being taught. Newspapers were published from the camps as well. In the camps, food and provisions were offered free of charge and at the same time Okinawans began to learn about the prosperity of Americans and about democracy.

On islands where the U.S. forces made no landings during the Battle of Okinawa, such as on the Yaeyama Islands, the residents began to build democratic organizations by themselves. But in December U.S. forces were stationed there and the rule of the military government began.

The Start of Postwar Government

The U.S. military government took note of the achievements of the Okinawa Advisory Council and in April of 1946 renamed it the Okinawa Civil Government and appointed Koshin Shikiya as governor of the civil government. They also established a legislature and appointed representatives. The political and administrative framework was made with the forceful intention of the U.S. military government. It was said that The U.S. military was the cat and Okinawa was the mouse. Another saying at the time was "The mouse can only play in the range the cat allows," and the civil rights of the residents were fairly confined.

In 1950 four Gunto districts were created; the Amami Islands Gunto, the Okinawa Islands Gunto, the Miyako Islands Gunto, and the Yaeyama Islands. Elections were held and governors were selected, but the wishes of the Okinawans were not at all reflected in the policies of the military government.

During this time, the U.S. military, having separated its occupation of Okinawa from that of mainland Japan, did not initiate any clear- cut policies due to the opposition of the U.S. State Department to permanent U.S. Bases on Okinawa. For this reason, Okinawa was termed the "forgotten island", progress was held in stasis, and confusion on the island continued.

In 1946, the postwar constitution was promulgated on the Japanese mainland and democratization of the nation began under occupation. However, in Okinawa the residents suffered through difficulties obtaining food, high- handedness of the U.S. soldiers, and restrictions on freedoms such as speech, assembly, and the right to self-government. In the midst of these conditions, Okinawans, together with those repatriated from the mainland, began the movement to expand autonomy .

In May 1947, the "Okinawa Kensetsu Kondankai," the first postwar island-wide political assembly, was held and a petition was submitted to the Okinawa Civil Administration Governor concerning demands for the establishment of an assembly that would reflect the will of the Okinawan people, an end to corruption, and a more equitable and adequate supply distribution system. Taking this opportunity, the Okinawa Democratic Union, the Okinawa People's Party, and the Okinawa Socialist Party were established. The military government recognized the local municipal elections for the assemblies and village and city mayors, but was unenthusiastic about the recognition of the election of a governor and an Okinawan assembly. Far from accepting, the reaction, the military authorities were autocratic and there were interruptions of supply deliveries, price hikes, and dissolution of the Okinawa Legislature in an attempt at suppression. This confrontation led to the growth of demands for self-government among the Okinawans.

Life under the U.S. Occupation

Around October 1945, permission was granted to move out of the internment camps and back into the villages and towns. But when residents returned to their villages, some found their land had been requisitioned as munitions or supply depots and they had no place to go.

The prewar system of municipalities and jurisdictions was revived, but it entailed starting from zero. Among the residents who were trying hard just to get food and supplies, the "fruits of war," black markets in stolen goods started forming and there were more than a few instances where persons stealing were shot at by U.S. troops.

In the middle part of 1946 there was still no currency available, so goods were bartered. There were several currency exchanges that occurred after this time but to prevent the inflation caused by the influx of Japanese yen, the military government introduced the B Yen currency, which provided a start for economic activities.

However, commodity prices, wages, and salaries were controlled so there were no free exchange transactions. This was when the black markets and smuggling goods became a major activity. In a life with so many restrictions, the residents of Okinawa constructed Sanshin (Okinawan samisen) from whatever was available, such as tin cans and string. They played and sang songs, prayed to their village gods, and tried to reconstruct Okinawa.

USCAR and the Struggle for Autonomous Rights

The Policy of Maj. Gen. Sheets and the Treaty of San Francisco

Early relief funding provided by the GARIOA (Government and Relief in Occupied Areas) was taken over by the LARA Program (Licensed Agencies for Relief in Asia) in 1949. This was the start of economic recovery in Okinawa.

The U.S. military placed Major General Joseph R. Sheets in command of the U.S. Directive Administration for Okinawa (RYCOM) as governor to oversee the restoration of order in the government. General Sheets planned for the permanent rule and construction of U. S. Military bases on Okinawa and accomplished a number of policies during his time. The policies he advocated were received by the Okinawans kindly and his term in office was widely regarded as "The Good Government of Sheets".

The first of his policies implemented as governor was the reorganization of the jumble of military facilities and facilities construction with a high degree of order and efficiency. In the next set of policies he set out to accomplish increasing the extent of social welfare systems. The third set of policies was the public recognition of self-rule, the reduction of military government on each of the island groups, and the implementation of elections for governor and members of an island-wide legislature. In December 1950, the American Far East Command issued orders for dissolution of the U. S. Military Government and the establishment of the United States Civil Administration of the Ryukyu Islands (USCAR).

In September of 1951, representatives from fifty-two nations gathered at U.S. invitation in San Francisco and opened a conference on the proposed peace treaty with Japan. Japan called for a universal peace treaty with all nations that it had fought with in WWII, including the Soviet Union and China. Prime Minister Shigeru Yoshida participated in the conference which resulted in the conclusion of a peace treaty with forty-eight of the participating countries. This was the San Francisco Peace Treaty.

In the 3rd article of the treaty, it stated the conditions of U.S. right to rule the Okinawa and Amami Islands. In three months time over 70% of the legal voters in Okinawa signed petitions in objection to this, but this was disregarded by both the Japanese and U.S. governments. Simultaneously, Japan concluded the Japan - U.S. Security Treaty. On April 28, 1952 both treaties took effect and Japan regained its independence.

Okinawa was separated from Japan and became the "Keystone of the Pacific," assuming an important and strategic place in U.S. policy in Asia.

The Establishment of the Government of the Ryukyus

In 1950, in the Gunto Island district governor elections, many of those elected had waged campaigns stressing the idea of reversion to Japan. In the reforms carried out within the political parties as a result of the elections, the promotion of reversion to Japan became part of the basic party platform of the Okinawa Socialist Masses Party (Shadaito).

After the election of the Gunto district governors, the U.S. government changed the administration of the islands from the military government to the three tiered United States Civil Administration of the Ryukyu Islands (USCAR). This federal system consisted of the Central Government, the Gunto Governments and the municipal city and village jurisdictions.

The U.S. by now had become aware of the reversion sentiments of the Gunto district governments and in April of 1951 established the Provisional Central Government to protect its legislative, judicial and administrative rights until a more permanent Central Government could be formed. With the appearance of the Provisional Central Government the Gunto governments became governments in name only.

In March of 1952 the residents of Okinawa voted in majority for candidates that were promoting the reversion to Japan in a direct election of the legislature. The U.S. Civil Administration sensed an impending crisis and, on April 1, appointed Shuhei Higa as the first chief executive of the Government of the Ryukyus Islands. The Gunto governments, elected by the people of Okinawa with their hopes in mind, were disbanded.

Okinawa as a Strategic Base

In Okinawa in the 1950's, the base expansion reached a peak of activity, a symbol of the rising tensions between the U.S. and the Soviet Union. Around the time the Treaty of San Francisco was concluded and the leased land contracts for the military bases advanced as well. Before that the land expropriated for military bases was used free of charge, but starting in 1946, the land ownership projects re-established land ownership and there were demands from the landowners for compensation.

With the conclusion of the treaty, the basis for the use of land without payments no longer applied and the establishment of leases became a necessity for the U.S. military. The U.S. Civil Administration promised to pay rent dated back to 1950. However, the rates were so low the resistance to them was extreme.

USCAR's expectations to conclude the leasing agreements were not met so it issued land acquisition procedures in April of 1953. Residents who refused to vacate expropriated land were forcibly evicted at bayonet point and the houses were bulldozed over.

This was how the large U.S. military bases appeared in Okinawa. The people who had lost their land were employed on the bases, but the industrial base was weak and the economy became distorted and consumption oriented.

The Price Report and the Island-wide Struggles

In March of 1954 the U.S. Civil Administration indicated it would issue land rents in one ten-year lump sum payment. In response to this, the elected legislature, in keeping with the will of the Okinawan residents, passed a resolution containing the "Four Principles of Land Protection." This was the start of island-wide protests.

The U.S. Civil Administration regarded the principles as unrealistic, ignored them, and continued their forcible expropriation of land. Increasingly resolute Okinawan resistance led the Government of the Ryukyus to dispatch a delegation in May 1955 to Washington to present the "Four Principles" directly to the American government. In response to the submission of the appeal from the delegation from Okinawa, a U.S. House of Representative committee dispatched a survey group headed by Senator Price to Okinawa.

The results of Senator Price's survey were presented to the U.S. Congress in the following year. It contained no mention of the Okinawan desire for reversion to Japan. It also contained details of the conditions of the U.S. rule in Okinawa and spoke of the desirability for a long term U.S. military presence in Okinawa. The report was a bitter disappointment to the Okinawans and throughout the islands groups gathered in protests. 1956 was the year when the "Island-wide Struggle" was ignited.

Toward these protests USCAR issued an off-limits order to military personnel forbidding their people access to civilian areas. This inflicted economic damage on Okinawa. As a result the Government of the Ryukyus recognized the use of land for the bases, the U.S. Civil Administration promised to award fair value for land use and the matter was finally settled

The Rise of the Popular Movement and Reversion
Damage from the Bases and Okinawan Human Rights

On June 30, 1959 a U.S. military jet crashed on Miyamori Elementary School in Ishikawa City and was reported worldwide as one of the worst tragedies in the history of aviation. Seventeen people were killed, eleven of them children, and 121 people were gravely injured. Twenty-five houses were burned. The U.S. military made a definite promise to compensate for the accident but it took them nearly three years to finally give payment.

During this period there were numerous incidents where the human rights of the Okinawans were disregarded by the U.S. military. There were also many problems relating to the legal judgements regarding crimes and accidents. Many of the accused were found not guilty and even in cases where guilt was established, perpetrators were sent back to the U.S. where the execution of sentences was obscured. Okinawan residents were forced to swallow the injustices.

There was further damage to the environment from live-fire exercises, pollution from nuclear-powered submarines, contamination of water supplies, wells, and soil from effluent waste from the bases. These became daily occurrences.

Under the rule of the U.S. military, the American military received all priority and the human rights of the Okinawans were ignored. The economic prosperity of the 1960's in Okinawa brought by the military bases was paid for in the danger to the lives of the Okinawans and the disregard for their basic rights.

The Rise of the People

On April 28, 1960 the Okinawa Teacher's Association, the Okinawa Prefecture Association of Youth Groups, and the Union of Government Employees of Okinawa acted as go-betweens in the organization of a nonpartisan group, The Okinawa Reversion Council, devoted to issues regarding the return of Okinawa to the mainland of Japan. Following this, activities for reversion were conducted but the U.S. Civil Administration enacted no changes in their rule over Okinawa.

If a situation occurred that was not to the convenience of USCAR, which held the real power within Okinawa, a decree or announcement was made and the demands of the residents were ignored or denied. In 1963 the High Commissioner, Lt. General Paul W. Caraway caused a stir with his pronouncements on the "Myth of Okinawan Autonomy" and the direct control of the U.S. Civil Administration over Okinawa came into view.

Under the rule of such a Hicom, dissatisfaction with the lack of will shown by the Government of the Ryukyus spread to all levels of Okinawan society. Civic activism shook the entirety of the Okinawa Islands with the aim of a return to Japan. The movement became the focus of international attention.

With the intensification of the Vietnam War in the 1960's, the U.S. military came under increasing criticism internationally and this caused great change. U.S. President Lyndon Johnson was pressed to cease the bombing of North Vietnam and the issue of an Okinawan reversion to Japan was taken up between the governments of Japan and the United States.

The Development of the Popular Movement

In the 1960's the land disputes had settled down to a certain degree, but issues regarding the bases continued to weigh heavily on Okinawans. The residents of Okinawa came to the recognition that these problems were derived from rule by a foreign country and the desire developed to abolish this domination, and return to Japan under it's constitution of peace. This spurred the movement toward reversion. Through this movement the struggle to force withdrawal of the "Twin Education Bills" and the establishment of direct election for the office of Chief Executive of the Government of the Ryukyus developed. The "Twin Education Bills" were aimed at controlling the civic activism of teachers.

The bills were entitled the "Regional Education District Public Employee Law" and the "Special Law for Public Employees in Education." Similar laws had already been effected in the mainland of Japan. They included the enactment of regulations on the political activity of educators and were taken as an attempt to smash the reversion movement that included the teaching unions. Resistance to these measures sprung up.

However, the power of the conservative Democratic Party was squarely behind passage of the bills and the debate split the unity of the Okinawans into two.

After numerous attempts to have the bill brought to a vote the conservatives forced a vote during the February Plenary session of the legislature. Over twenty thousand attended a demonstration in front of the Legislature building in support of the teachers and the bill was withdrawn. With the backdrop of the mass demonstration outside the Legislature, the minority party of the Legislature got withdrawal of the bill and received great praise from all quarters.

Close of the Return to Japan Movement and Okinawan Reversion

When Japanese Prime Minister Eisaku Sato visited Okinawa in 1965 he stated that "The postwar era will not end so long as Okinawa is not returned." However, the terms of reversion as advocated bilaterally by Japan and the U.S. and those sought by the Okinawan people were quite divergent in nature.

The Okinawan Reversion movement began to resist the rule of a foreign nation and as civic activism to unify with their ethnic group. After the protests against the "Twin Education Bills" in the latter half of the 1960's, the struggle, which had begun by waving the Hinomaru flag of Japan as a symbol, shifted emphasis for unification with their ethnic group toward being anti-war and pacifist.

In 1968 in the elections for the Chief Executive of the Government of the Ryukyus, Chobyo Yara, a candidate that stressed "immediate, unconditional, and complete reversion" soundly beat out the other candidate and won the office of Chief Executive. The defeated Junji Nishime had also stressed unification with Japan. Also in 1970, the enactment of a bill in the Japanese Diet allowed elected representatives from Okinawa participation in the Diet. The resulting election saw victory for the Reformist candidates and indicated the hopes of the Okinawan people in a removal of the military bases from Okinawa.

In November of 1969, the talks between Japanese Prime Minister Sato and U.S. President Nixon resulted in a joint declaration of a "non-nuclear Okinawa, one of parity with Japan, and reversion in 1972". Opposition to the details of the agreement caused widespread protest among the Okinawan people.

Okinawan Culture under U.S. Military Rule

Due to the fierceness of the Battle of Okinawa, many of the superb cultural legacies created during the Ryukyu Kingdom Era were lost or destroyed. Gathering up the scattered and lost pieces of this cultural heritage became the start of Okinawa's cultural reconstruction.

The U.S. military expressed understanding of the collection of cultural artifacts. The residents of Shuri collected the cultural properties scattered about and in 1946 opened the Shuri City Folk Museum, which became the Shuri Museum the following year. In 1945 the U.S. military opened the Okinawa Display Hall in the Higashionna area of Ishikawa City . The following year this became the Higashionna Folk Museum.

In May 1953 these museums were consolidated into the Museum of the Government of the Ryukyu Islands, which at present has become the Okinawa Prefectural Museum. In the 1950's the cultural properties were restored and reconstructed. The Sunu-hiyan Utaki Ishimon Stone Gate and Shureimon Gate in Shuri were reconstructed.

The U.S. Civil Administration also established the Ryukyu Cultural Hall and the Ryukyu Friendship Center as facilities for exchange between the Okinawan people and Americans. The educational system was started in the internment camps after the war but a 6-year elementary, a 3-year junior high and 3 year senior high school system was implemented in 1948. In 1950 the University of the Ryukyus was founded on the site of the ruined Shuri Castle.

The field of literature began again. Taking themes from their lives resisting the rule of a foreign nation, writers Tatsuhiro Oshiro and Mineo Higashi both won the prestigious Akutagawa Prize for Literature. In the areas of music and the performing arts, Ryukyuan music and Ryukyuan Dance experienced a great resurgence. The youth of Okinawa took to the jazz and rock they heard from the servicemen on the bases and a new generation of active musicians was fostered. The mixture of jazz, rock, and traditional Okinawan folk songs resulted in the birth of Okinawan Music.

The Phases of Pre-Reversion Okinawa

In November 1968, immediately after the elections for Chief Executive called for by massive public activism, a number of base-related accidents occurred. First, a U.S. B-52 bomber crashed on take-off from Kadena Airfield and then a munition carrier crashed and overturned nearby. Okinawa during that period was an embarkation point for U.S. troops heading to Vietnam and the B-52s routinely took off for bombing runs to Vietnam. This was the context in which the Okinawan mass movements for pacifism and against war developed.

In 1970, at year's end, an accident occurred where a car driven by a U.S. soldier struck an Okinawan crossing an intersection in Nakanomachi, Koza City (Okinawa City). Residents, feeling resentment at the frequency of these incidents and the unfair handling of such cases, exploded with anti-U.S. sentiment and rioted. Over seventy cars were burned that night in the so-called Koza Riot.

This affair, occurring as it did in a town dependent on the U.S. military bases and by people regarded as obedient by the military authorities, came as a big shock to the American military. It also influenced the negotiations for reversion of Okinawa that were taking place between Japan and the United States.

The talks for reversion involving governments of both countries ignored the Okinawan people's hope for a non-nuclear island of peace and continued laying the foundation for a continued base presence on Okinawa. The Reversion Council decried the "Agreement between Japan and the United States concerning the Ryukyu Islands and the Daito Islands" and carried out general strikes throughout Okinawa.

Without concern for these events, the governments of Japan and the United States concluded the agreement with a joint signing in Tokyo and Washington in June 1971. The decisions made regarding the conditions of reversion ignored the demands of the Okinawan people. Okinawans, wanting a revision of the reversion agreement before ratification in the Diet, staged a massive demonstration calling for re-negotiation. However, despite the petitions brought to Tokyo by Chief

Executive Yara the reversion agreement was forcibly voted on in the Diet.

The New Life of Okinawa

Rebirth of Okinawa Prefecture

In January 1972 Japanese Prime Minister Sato and American President Nixon held consultations and decided on May 15, 1972 as the day of reversion.

The Government of the Ryukyus established the "People's Council on Restoration Issues" to advise the Chief Executive. They studied summaries of the reversion policies of both Japan and America. Chief Executive Chobyo Yara received the report and petitioned both governments, finally writing a petition submitted to an extraordinary session of the Diet entitled the "Recommendations Regarding Reversion" emphasizing the theme of "immediate, unconditional, and complete reversion." On the day of submission of the recommendations a vote was forced on the reversion agreement and it was approved by the Diet.

On May15, 1972, after twenty-seven years of U.S. rule the islands of Okinawa reverted back to Japan. The terms of reversion were a far cry from the hopes of the residents of Okinawa, but, return to the sovereignty of the nation of Japan but reversion was none the less accomplished.

To start the new life of Okinawa Prefecture the Japanese government held commemorative services in Tokyo and Okinawa. The Tokyo ceremonies were held at the Budokan and Prime Minister Sato, U.S. Vice-President Agnew, and Lt. Gen. J. P. Lampert were in attendance. The ten thousand people there celebrated the new life of Okinawa Prefecture.

In Okinawa Prefecture the ceremonies included an address by Governor Yara, a man who had experienced the full bitterness involved with this day because of the various issues surrounding the reversion, including those of the U.S. military bases on Okinawa.

The Okinawa Reversion Council, which had promoted the reversion effort, opened a general meeting in Naha's Yogi Koen Park on the day of reversion and adopted a resolution opposing the reversion. On the other hand, the Okinawa Executive committee organized a celebratory meeting in Naha City on the night before the reversion

Special Reversion Measures and Life of the Prefectural Citizens

Life for the citizens of Okinawa changed greatly after reversion to mainland Japan. One of the first things was the currency shift from dollars to yen. The dollar was low against the yen at the time of reversion. The Japanese government decided that was a loss of profit for the Okinawans and promised to exchange dollars at the rate of 360 yen to the dollar, with the difference in the real rate to be compensated by the Japanese government. But, because of various related problems and because of price hikes, consumer prices rose 14.5% in one month.

In order to smooth the change in the economy of Okinawa after twenty-seven years of separate development from the economic and political system of the mainland, the government devised the Special Reversion Measures. According to these measures, the Okinawa Development Agency was to formulate plans every ten years for Okinawa's promotion and development in order to correct the disparities between the mainland and Okinawa. This public fund was established to maintain the roads, harbors and agriculture, and gradually the income of the prefecture's citizens grew.

As projects commemorating the reversion, in November 1972 the Planting Festival to Commemorate Reversion was held, in May of 1973 the Okinawa Special National Athletic Meet (the Wakanatsu Games) were held, and starting in July of 1975 for half a year, the Okinawa International Ocean Exposition was held.

On July 30,1978 the traffic patterns changed to the left to meet Japanese standards in the "People to the right, Cars to the Left" campaign.

Keywords in Postwar Okinawa

Yaka Horyo Shuyou-jo (Yaka POW Camp)

Located in the Yaka district of Kin-cho village, the internment camp was a large-scale facility for Imperial Japanese Army prisoners after the war. There were 7,000 prisoners housed here, including 5,000 Japanese troops. The remaining were Koreans and Okinawan-born soldiers.

Okinawa Shijun-kai (Okinawa Advisory Council)

Established by the U.S. Military Government, the Advisory Council was an intermediate organization paving the way for the establishment of the central government. There were 15 members consisting mostly of educators and media people. Koshin Shikiya was chosen as council chair.

Okinawa Min Seifu (Okinawa Civil Government)

In 1946 the Okinawa Advisory Council became the Okinawa Civil

Government at the same time as the establishment of the Okinawa Legislature. Koshin Shikiya was appointed the first governor.

Gunto Governments

The Okinawa Civil Government was composed of four districts; Amami, Okinawa, Miyako, and Yaeyama. In 1950 these were reorganized and called Gunto Governments, and governors and legislature members from each area were chosen by elections. The will of the people was not reflected into the policy areas of the military government.

Senka (Fruits of War)

In Okinawa under U.S. military rule, provisions were given by America but the people still suffered under chronic food shortages. For that reason there were many who stole stores from the depots of the U.S. military which they named the "Fruits of War."

B Yen Currency

The yen currency in circulation before the war was exchanged for equivalent B Yen currency issued by the U.S. Military Government. For a short time after the war this currency was used simultaneously with the new yen issued by the Japanese. From 1948 to 1958 the introduction and circulation of the new Japanese yen was prohibited and the B-yen was the only legal currency in use in Okinawa.

Mitsu Boueki (Smuggling)

Smuggling flourished under U.S. military occupation. Metal debris left over from the Battle of Okinawa such as used artillery shells was shipped to Taiwan or Hong Kong to be exchanged for everyday commodities. American medical supplies were transported to mainland Japan and exchanged for pots, pans, and tableware. Particularly in areas such as the Miyako and Yaeyama regions, where the aid from the American military was late in arriving,, the practice of smuggling is said to have flourished. Textbooks, notepads, and even copies of the Peace Constitution entered Okinawa in this way. Doing this to survive showed the wisdom of the people and their initiative.

Kankara Sanshin (Okinawan samisen made from tin cans)

Having lost all in the war and surrounded by the anxiety of postwar life, the people of Okinawa placed their spirit in singing and playing the Sanshin. Since there were no satisfactory instruments around, the empty cans from the provisions handed out, sticks, and the string from parachutes were assembled into instruments like the Karakan Sanshin.

Sheets Policies

Maj. Gen. Joseph R. Sheets oversaw preparation and construction of the military facilities and bases on Okinawa. His policies also included the authorization of land rights, the discharge of unneeded land used by the military, the promotion of building private sector enterprises, establishment of bus services, and improvements in educational facilities. Maj. Gen. Sheets promoted the realization of postwar reconstruction in Okinawa. His tour of duty in Okinawa also resulted in the establishment of the University of the Ryukyus. He aggressively tackled the comprehensive organizational reforms, established the Ryukyu Military Headquarters, which ruled each of the Gunto district military governments, and reshuffled the military service members that were embroiled in the resistance of the residents of Okinawa. He reduced the power of the Gunto district military governments that had become a hindrance to the self-autonomy of the Okinawans.

However, despite being termed the " Good Governor Sheets," he laid the groundwork of his policies on the construction of the military bases and a permanent U.S. military presence and rule in Okinawa.

United States Civil Administration of the Ryukyu Islands

The U.S. government believed that a central government was needed to rule over the four Gunto district governments and so changed control of the ruling organization in Okinawa from the military government to the United States Civil Administration of the Ryukyu Islands (USCAR). The U.S. Civil Administration's business was handled by the officer in command of the Ryukyu Military Headquarters, who worked as Deputy Governor of the U.S. Civil Administration.

The Reversion of Amami Shoto Islands

The Amami Island Group was also separated from Japan after the end of WWII and came under U.S. military rule. The residents on the Amami Islands developed their own movement for reversion. Over 99.8% of the people signed petitions for reversion and they received over three hundred thousand signatures from mainland residents. They opened large protest rallies, and appealed to the United Nations and the U.S. president in a broad international effort for reversion. On December 25, 1953 Amami was returned to the mainland of Japan after eight years of U.S. government rule.

The Government of the Ryukyus Islands

Established under the will of the U.S. Civil Administration, the Government of the Ryukyus was a self-governing body with legislative, judicial and administrative rights. In terms of political power it was provisioned to exercise full power over the Ryukyus but, in actuality, it had to act in accordance with the U.S. Civil Administration and Ryukyu Military Headquarters.

Compulsory Land Expropriation

In order for the U.S. Civil Administration to conclude leases for the vast land it was using as bases, it promulgated its "right to lease" in November 1952. But the rental rates for the land were extremely low, about the cost of a bottle of cola for 29.7 square meters (9 tsubo) and the term of lease was twenty years. Many landowners did not respond. The lack of response prompted the U.S. Civil Administration to issue land expropriation laws in 1953, enabling it to unilaterally acquire land without the need for signed leases. It was an unreasonable and extraordinary measure to seize land from the residents.

Bayonets and Bulldozers

This term came into use to express the methods the U.S. military used to forcibly expropriate land. They expelled those who resisted eviction at bayonet point and, without allowing them to move out their goods, destroyed their houses with bulldozers.

Tokuju (Special Procurement)

This term usually meant a request for goods or services, excepting trade, made by the U.S. military. It helped the recovery of the sluggish domestic economy and allowed the Japanese economy to develop greatly. The building of the military bases was contracted out mainly to mainland Japanese construction companies as well as those from America, Hong Kong, Taiwan, and Okinawa. In the case of the Japanese construction companies the government aggressively financed them and they occupied greater than half of those doing the construction and reaped great profits.

The Four Principles of Land Protection

After receiving the U.S. Civil Administration's announcement of lump sum payments for land use, the Legislature unanimously passed a resolution concerning "Petitions Relating to the Processing of Military Land." The details of the resolution came to known as "The Four Principles of Land Protection" and are as follows: 1. No lump sum payments, 2. Payment of appropriate compensation, 3. Payment for damages incurred from the U.S. military, and 4. Opposition to new land expropriation.

The Price Recommendations

In response to the submission of petitions from the delegation from Okinawa, a U.S. House of Representatives Armed Services committee dispatched Senator Melvin Price and a survey group to Okinawa. After only three days of observation the group returned home and issued a report stating the importance of the Okinawan military bases to the U.S. military in the Far East. For the Okinawans the report did not recognize the movement for self-rule, allowed the possibility of the bases for long-term use, and placed no limitations on the storage of nuclear weapons and the use of land by a foreign government. The recommendations were a shock to the hopes of the people because the report supported lump sum payments and new land expropriation to secure absolute ownership rights for U.S. military bases.

Off Limits

Off Limits decrees issued by the U.S. military prohibited U.S. servicemen, personnel and their families from going into civilian areas of Okinawa. They were decreed as a way to avoid trouble because of the protests and demonstrations staged by the Okinawans. However, it carried grave economic repercussions on a region with an economy that was dependent on the U.S. bases. The issuance of an Off Limits order was a cause of anxiety, particularly in the central region of mainland Okinawa with its concentration of bases.

The crash of a U.S. military jet on Miyamori Elementary School

On June 30, 1959 tragedy occurred when a U.S. military jet aircraft crashed on the Miyamori Elementary School in Ishikawa City, killing seventeen people including eleven children, seriously injuring 121 persons and setting fire to 25 homes. The pilot ejected before the crash and was unharmed. The U.S. military declared it to be an unavoidable accident and promised adequate compensation but final settlement took close to three years.

Vietnam War

Before the war Vietnam was a colony of France but Japan occupied it for fifteen years during the war. Afterwards, the country was divided between the Socialist Republic of Vietnam (North Vietnam) and Vietnam (South Vietnam). France, America, Great Britain and others actively intervened in support of the south. Kadena military base in Okinawa became an important station for the sorties, logistics, and dispatch of troops to the battlefields.

The Myth of Autonomy

High Commissioner Lt. General Paul W. Caraway exercised absolute power and caused a whirlwind with his comments such as "Currently autonomy is a myth - it doesn't exist. And until the people of the Ryukyus decide that they once again wish to be a sovereign nation, there will be no autonomy in the future either."

The Fukkikyo (Reversion Council)

The Okinawa Reversion to the Fatherland Council (shortened to Fukkikyo in Japanese) conducted reversion activities every year on the day of separation from Japan, April 28, 1952. To the council it was "Humiliation Day" and they held protest activities on this date after that.

Transfer of Jurisdiction Protest

In 1966, under the order of High Commissioner Albert Watson, jurisdiction in two lawsuits, "The Mackerel Case" and the "Tomori Election Case," both involving orders issued by the U.S. Civil Administration, were transferred from the Ryukyu Court of Appeals to the U.S. Civil Administration Courts. The Ryukyuan Court responded to the order for transfer, but due to the increasing demands for autonomy from the Okinawan residents, the Legislature adopted a resolution calling for the order for transfer of jurisdiction to be rescinded. High Commissioner Watson paid no heed to the resolution and was in command at the judgement. The court decision by the Ryukyuan Court recognized the decision of the U.S. Civil Administration Court decision and victory in the election was awarded to Tomori. Later the High Commissioner was changed.

Twin Education Bill Protest

The "Twin Education Bills" refer to two bills, the "Regional Education District Public Employee Law" and the "Special Law for Public Employees in Education." They clarified the legal position of regional public employees and guaranteed their positions. Parts of the bills concerning teachers implemented evaluations, restricted political activities and prohibited the participation in strikes. The teacher's unions, joined by other groups, saw this as an attempt to destroy the reversion movement and opposed the law.

The Koza Riot

Past 11:00 o'clock on the evening of December 19, 1970 a U.S. soldier driving across an intersection hit an Okinawan. The residents of the area protested because they believed the case was being handled by the Military Police unfairly. Warning shots fired by the MPs to discourage the crowd resulted in an explosion of anti-American sentiment. The angry crowd overturned vehicles of Americans and set them on fire. Police and soldiers in full battle gear were called out to quell the disturbance, but it lasted six hours and resulted in the burning of seventy-three U.S. vehicles. Some in the crowd entered areas attached to Kadena Military Base and burnt three buildings down including an office and a U. S. elementary school.

Toxic Gas Transport

On July 8, 1969 there was an accidental leakage of toxic gas from a munitions storage facility in the Chibana section of central Okinawa Island. Twenty-four U.S. servicemen were hospitalized with sickness from it and the event was kept secret. Personnel in the area related to the military, unhappy with the incident, revealed the accident to the media. In response to questions about the incident made by Chief

Executive Yara, High Commissioner Lampert stated that the injuries were of an extremely minor nature.

A few days later the U.S. State Department confirmed that deadly gasses such as Sarin and Mustard gas were being stored in Okinawa, which caused reaction both domestically and internationally. Protest for the removal of the gas from Okinawa resulted in it being transferred to U.S. Territory on Johnston Island.

In January of 1971 the U.S. military began transport of the gas to Tengan Pier. During that period of time, 5,000 residents along the passage took refuge.

The CTS Facilities

The CTS oil storage facility was brought to Okinawa in hopes of promoting industry and expanding employment. The effects on employment were slight and the accidental discharge of crude oil caused environmental pollution. Massive protests criticized its construction.

Junji Nishime

The conservative administration of Governor Nishime lasted from 1978 to 1990. The characteristics of his administration were a retreat from U.S. military base policies and an emphasis on regional development and international exchange. The Nishime administration's policies resulted in the gradual economic growth for Okinawa Prefecture, but were heavily dependent on public financing and the industrial structure inclined, in the extreme, toward tertiary industries without developing a self-sustaining economy capable of vitalizing the region.

The Cornerstone of Peace

As a memorial project for the 50th anniversary of the ending of the Battle of Okinawa, the Cornerstone of Peace was erected in the Peace Memorial Park in Itoman City. The memorial walls are inscribed with the names of all combatants and civilians, without regard to nationality, that died in the Battle of Okinawa.

Sexual Assault Incident on a Young Okinawan Girl

In September of 1995 a rape incident involving a sexual assault on a young girl by three U.S. military personnel occurred. When requested to turn over the suspects to the prefectural police, the U.S. military refused immediate turnover of the suspects based on the Status of Forces Agreement between Japan the United States. The Ministry of Foreign Affairs also indicated reluctance and there were demands from Okinawa Prefecture and the Okinawa Prefectural Legislature for a re-evaluation of the Status of Forces Agreement, but both the Japanese government and the Foreign Ministry declined. This ignited long unresolved problems surrounding the U.S. bases on Okinawa and led to the massive protest rally in 1995.

Proxy Signature Judgment

When the leases of landowners of property on U.S. bases expired, some refused to renew the lease agreements as an anti-war protest. When this happens, the mayor of the municipality or governor can sign the lease as proxy. However Governor Ota refused to sign the leases as proxy and the Prime Minister filed a lawsuit to enforce execution of the proxy order by the governor. The case was tried in the Supreme Court with the prefectural side losing the appeal of the case.

Prefectural Citizen's Referendum

Japan's first citizen's referendum was held on the issue of "Consolidation and Reduction of the U.S. military bases on Okinawa and a revision of the Status of Forces Agreement." The voting rate did not exceed the expected 60% of the voting public but an overwhelming majority supported the calls for reducing the bases and revision of the SOFA agreement.

SACO (The Japan-U.S. Special Action Committee on Okinawa)

This is a special committee set up concerning facilities and districts in Okinawa in order to discuss base cutbacks and consolidation. It was established in November of 1995 with a one-year mandate from the Japan-U.S. Security Commission.

Okinawa Prefectural Citizen's General Protest

This was a large general protest rally held on October 21, 1995 to denounce the sexual assault of a young girl by U.S. military personnel and to demand revision of the Status of Forces Agreement. It is said over 85,000 prefectural citizens participated and was the largest protest rally in post reversion Okinawa

King Houghton

Tourism in Okinawa Information

The prefecture of Okinawa comprises more than one hundred islands, stretching over 700km of ocean from Kyushu southwest to Yonaguni-jima, almost within sight of Taiwan. Collectively known as the Ryukyu Shoto , this chain of subtropical islands, with their lush vegetation, paradise beaches and superb coral reefs, has become a popular destination for Japanese holiday-makers and foreign residents alike. Few other tourists make it down here, partly because of the time and cost involved, but if you've had your fill of shrines and temples, want to check out some of Japan's best beaches and dive sites , or simply fancy a spot of winter sun, then Okinawa is well worth considering.

The largest island in the group, Okinawa-Honto , usually referred to simply as Okinawa, is the region's transport hub and home to its prefectural capital, Naha . It's also the most heavily populated and developed of the Ryukyu chain, thanks largely to the controversial presence of American military bases . While it's the remoter islands that are worth concentrating on - particularly the Yaeyama group centred around Ishigaki-jima - Okinawa-Honto boasts a number of historical sights, many of them associated with the Battle of Okinawa at the end of the Pacific War. But the island has more to offer, particularly in its northern region, where the old way of life still survives among the isolated villages.

To see the best of the region, you have to hop on a plane or ferry and explore the dozens of outer islands, many of which are uninhabited. Even quite close to Naha, you'll find gorgeous beaches and fantastic dive spots around the Kerama islands, just 30km off the main island. Divers and beach connoisseurs will want to visit Miyako-jima and Ishigaki-jima, way down the Ryukyu chain, where tiny star-shaped shells dust the sand. If you're looking for an idyllic retreat, Taketomi-jima can't be beaten, while the adventurous will want to explore Iriomote-jima, coated in thick groves of mangrove and steamy rainforest and home to the elusive Iriomote lynx.

It's on these outer islands that you'll also find the strongest evidence of the much-vaunted Ryukyu culture, born of contact with Taiwan and China, as well as Japan. The most obvious features are different types of food a vibrant use of colour, and bold, tropical patterns, while the Chinese influence is clearly visible in the architecture, traditional dress and the martial art of karate - the Ryukyu warriors preferred mode of protection. Ancient religious beliefs are kept alive by shamen (called *yuta*) and, on Okinawa-Honto, there are sumo bouts between bulls. There's also a Ryukyu dialect, with dozens of variations between the different islands, unique musical instruments, and a distinctive musical style which has captured an international audience through bands such as Nenes, Diamantes and Champloose. If you're lucky, you'll stumble on a local festival, such as giant rope tug-of-war contests or dragon-boat races, while the biggest annual event is the *Eisa* festival (15th of the seventh lunar month) when everyone downs tools and dances to the incessant rhythms of drums, flutes and the three-stringed *sanshin* .

Those in search of local crafts will find beautiful *Bingata* textiles the most appealing. Originally reserved for court ladies, *Bingata* fabrics are hand-dyed with natural pigments from hibiscus flowers and various vegetables, in simple but striking patterns. Also worth searching out are the fine *jofu* cloths of Miyako-jima and the Yaeyama Islands, once gifted in tribute to the local monarchs. Ceramics are thought to have been introduced to the region from Spain and Portugal in the fifteenth century, but Ryukyu potters concentrated on roof tiles and fairly rustic utensils. Nowadays, they churn out thousands of sake flasks and *shiisa* - the ferocious lion figures that glare down at you from every rooftop. The exquisite local lacquerware has a long history in the islands, too, having been introduced over 500 years ago from China, but the glassware you'll find is much more recent: it's said production took off in the postwar years when Okinawans set about recycling the drinks bottles of the occupying US forces.

Besides Hokkaido, Okinawa contains Japan's largest areas of unspoilt natural environment and greatest biodiversity. Much of this wealth of wildlife is underwater, spawned by the warm Kuroshio current that sweeps up the east coast and allows coral reefs to flourish. But on land, too, there are a number of unique species, including turtles, a crested eagle and the noguchigera (Pryer's woodpecker), in addition to Iriomote's wild cat, the yamaneko. A less welcome local resident is the highly poisonous habu snake . It measures around 2m in length, is dark green with a yellow head, and usually lurks in dense vegetation or on roadsides, though rarely ventures into urban areas. As long as you're careful - especially during spring and autumn - you should have no problems, but if you are bitten, make for the nearest hospital where they should have anti-venom.

With its subtropical climate , Okinawa stays warm throughout the year. Average annual temperatures are around 23°C, with a winter average of 17°C and a minimum of 10°C. Winter lasts from December through February, while the hot, humid summer starts in April and continues into September. Temperatures at this time hover around 34°C and the sun can be pretty intense, though the sea breezes help. The best time to visit is in spring or autumn, roughly March to early May and late September to December. The rainy season lasts from early May to early June, while typhoons can be a problem in July and August, and occasionally into October.

One of the more unusual ways of getting to Okinawa - and Japan - is to take the international ferry from Taiwan via Ishigaki and Miyako islands to Naha . By far the majority of visitors, however, arrive by plane. Most come from the Japanese mainland, though there are international flights to Naha from Taiwan, Korea and Hong Kong. Domestic airlines operate between Naha and Tokyo, Osaka and a number of other Japanese cities , while a few fly direct to Ishigaki and Miyako. Though flying can be expensive, discounts are becoming increasingly common, so it's always worth asking the airlines and travel agents. Overseas visitors can also take advantage of the airpasses offered by JAL and ANA .

The other option is a local ferry from Tokyo, Osaka, Kobe or one of several cities on Kyushu. All of these services stop in Naha, from where some continue to Miyako and Ishigaki . These ferries can be a great way to travel if you're not in a hurry, though horribly crowded in the peak summer season.

Getting around between islands presents a similar choice between air and sea, with Naha as the main hub. Inter-island flights are operated by Japan Transocean Air (JTA), Ryukyu Air Commuter (RAC) and Air Nippon (ANK), with connections to all the major islands. The ferry network, on the other hand, fans out from Naha's three terminals to every corner of the prefecture, allowing you to island-hop at your leisure. See individual island accounts for more about these sailings.

www.ingramcontent.com/pod-product-compliance
Lightning Source LLC
Chambersburg PA
CBHW021106080526
44587CB00010B/401